life balance

A Life-Balance Approach To
Reaching Your Goals and
Changing Your Life

Paul W. Croswell

life
balance

A Life-Balance Approach To
Reaching Your Goals and
Changing Your Life

PAUL W. CROSWELL

I dedicate this book to the two most important women in my life, my wife and my mother.

CONTENTS

A **Small** Step

In The **Right**

Direction Is A

Big Deal!

Introduction

"Be at war with your vices, at peace with your neighbors, and let every
new year find you a better person."

— Benjamin Franklin

One Saturday afternoon when I was eight years old, I noticed
an odd pain in my chest while playing with my cousins. Young and
naïve, I assumed it was a result of all the running we had done and
thought if I sat down for a while, it would dissipate. I was wrong.

Not only did the pain not go away, it worsened. After just a
few minutes, I had severe shortness of breath and throbbing chest
pain. I could barely move. My aunt quickly noticed that I was not as
mobile as normal and came to investigate. As I struggled through
my difficulty breathing to describe what I felt, it was clear from my
aunt's facial expression that it was serious.

Within minutes, we were on our way to the emergency room

and, after a brief examination, I was quickly admitted. The doctors explained that one of my lungs had completely collapsed, and the other was functioning at half capacity. They were certain that if my aunt hadn't rushed me in, I would have died within the next hour. Her vigilance saved my life. I was used to episodes of pain from sickle cell anemia, which I was diagnosed with at six months old, but I had never experienced something like this as a result of it before.

Addressing my anemic episode ended up requiring an extended stay in the Pediatric Intensive Care Unit, including a short time in which I was placed in a medically-induced coma. An experimental drug that hadn't been released to the market yet was used to treat me, and the doctors were unsure it would be successful. The entire ordeal could be summarized as nothing short of a miracle, and it taught me a powerful lesson about life. This traumatizing experience taught me the importance of intentional living.

This near-death incident underscored just how valuable our time is because life is so unpredictable, and that's a lesson I never took for granted after my time in the hospital. Ever since that experience I have kept a simple promise to myself: to live intentionally and make the most of life through the goals I set. I certainly haven't perfected the art of intentional living just yet, but I've learned a lot.

Over time, I found that a person's intentionality in life is most clearly reflected through the goals they set for themselves, their loved ones and friends, and even their jobs. However, setting goals and reaching them are two very different tasks. Many people have amazing goals that have the potential to transform their lives and the lives of many others, but struggle to reach them.

A series of studies done by the University of Scranton on New Year's resolutions found that only 19% of people were able to keep their resolutions long term. Almost 80% of the participants in their study quit on their goals after only one week.1 What's the lifespan of a new goal in your life?

THE POWER OF A GOAL

The goals you set are often mental pictures of a happier, healthier future for yourself and the people you love. These goals are also catalytic for making healthy decisions that move you in the direction of these brighter futures. There is also no way to tell just how far-reaching your goals are in their impact on the world.

Your desires to finish that degree, start that business, or take back control of your physical and mental health aren't just good ideas, they are a vital part of a flourishing life and improving our world. Finishing that degree may be the move that brings your family out of poverty. Starting that business may be the key to spending quality time with your growing children, not to mention how it might change the lives of your future employees for the better. Taking back control of your health now could make the difference between playing with your grandkids, or only being able to watch them play.

Goals like these are life-altering and often impact more people than we can imagine. So why would we quit on them? What makes it so easy for us to walk away from the life-changing benefits of achieving our goals?

There is a plethora of answers to this question, but here's an uncommon one—most peoples' decision to quit on their goals is rooted not in fear or indiscipline, but in a lack of life balance. An imbalanced life is a graveyard for even the simplest of goals. The chaos of constant, unanticipated, or mismanaged demands quickly buries new goals under waves of seemingly urgent attention-seeking issues.

Additionally, the impact of the career demands of the average working professional is altogether unnerving. *Harvard Business Review* reports that the United States spends more than 190 billion dollars annually in healthcare to address the physical and psychological effects of burnout.[2] That's the exact amount that the Australian government plans to spend over the next *decade* on boosting their defense.[3] To look at it differently, that's more than 15 billion dollars *monthly*, 4 billion dollars *weekly*, and an alarming 500 million dollars *daily* spent on the health impact of burnout. This is no cheap issue and its price goes beyond our finances.

Another survey reveals that Americans take 26% of their

work home.[4] This means that in addition to working long hours at the office, we now allow work to blend into our leisure and family time. Keep in mind that these statistics only reflect the work or career portion of life and do not account for the demands of our personal, family, or social lives. Under these circumstances, it is no surprise that new goals tend to have short lifespans. But what if it didn't have to be this way?

A LIFE-BALANCED APPROACH

What if there were a way to improve your life balance while fail-proofing your goals? A way of approaching goal-setting and goal-getting that honors the complicated nature of your life, your schedule, and your mental wiring? That's what this book is all about.

I discovered this approach over the course of eight years and multiple professions. In that time, I had a professional music career, started and led an independent record label, and worked as a pastor to young adults and teens at a large church. In each of these fields, the potential for being overwhelmed by unrealistic demands and schedules lived just beneath the surface. If this weren't enough, I also had to navigate sickle cell anemia, which, as I shared before, has its own demands.

Living *intentionally* was a must for me if I was to maintain a sense of balance in life, but I needed to learn how to live intentionally as a young professional with marriage and career responsibilities. So I did. I buried myself in books, explored different tools, and sought out mentors to help me grow in and master this idea of intentional living. Bearing in mind that losing balance in my life had severe consequences on my health, I was a highly motivated student.

So how does this relate to reaching goals? *I'm glad you asked!* At every point in my journey, my goals were massive, but my obstacles were many. Demanding and full schedules, health issues, and mental health obstacles, some of which I was unaware of, are just some of the things I needed to overcome to reach my goals.

To assist me in my journey, I started developing my own tools for managing work-life balance and reaching my goals through intentional living. These tools incorporated the principles I've learned over the years that kept me focused but also allowed me to be realistic about the demands of life. In this book, I share with you the life-balanced approach to reaching your goals by giving you access to the same tools and principles that helped me along the way.

THE THREE PARTS

The life-balanced approach is broken down into three parts: The Mental Battle, Taking Action, and Maintaining Success. This is a strategic way of thinking about how you achieve your goals. Each of the three parts is made up of four principles, each of which will be unpacked in detail.

Using the life-balanced approach, you will discover the qualities of an effective goal and explore the role of relationships on the journey toward your goals. You will also gain a greater understanding of the psychology of habit formation and the importance of brain health as it relates to your goals. Understanding the connectedness of each of these ideas equips you to maintain life balance and allows you to achieve true transformation through the goals you set.

1. **THE MENTAL BATTLE**: Every journey starts in the mind and heart before you ever take the first step. This section of the book is focused on helping you prepare to win the mental battle before you start your journey.

2. **TAKING ACTION**: How you take action toward your goals is vital and can make or break your ability to reach them. This section of the book will introduce a new way of seeing and going after your goals that exponentially increases your goal-reaching abilities.

3. **MAINTAINING SUCCESS**: Reaching your goal is not the end of your journey. This section of the book equips you with the principles necessary for maintaining long-term success. After all, no one wants to be the lottery winner who ends up broke after a year or two.

Regardless of where you are on your journey or what your success rate has been in the past, this approach can revolutionize your life balance and, subsequently, your ability to reach your goals and change your life. Keep in mind that this is not a magic formula and will still require that you show up and do the work, but if you can commit to showing up, I promise that you will find transformation on the other side.

ADDITIONAL RESOURCES

In addition to this book, I also created a free companion workbook to help you apply each of the principles we discuss. In this book, you will find a few questions to get you started, but the workbook contains complete exercises that help you to anchor each principle in action, which helps you to see your growth as you read. To maximize the potential of the principles you will learn, I highly recommend having the companion workbook. You can download your workbook at www.paulwcroswell.com/LifeBalanceResources.

Throughout this book, you will also learn about VIDA map, the life balance manager I designed with the principles of this book in mind. I'm excited to share this tool with you, and I hope you find it helpful in your journey to a healthier future. That said, let's fail-proof your goals!

Part One

How To Win The Mental Battle

PART ONE OVERVIEW

HOW TO WIN THE MENTAL BATTLE

The first step to reaching your goals and changing your life is winning the mental battle. You know the one. It's the mental battle that begins at the very moment you set your mind on a goal, as if just waiting for its moment to shine. We are all familiar with this battle, unfortunately, and you probably had to fight it again as you started this book.

This battle is made up of the barrage of negative thoughts and reminders of past failures at similar goals. Thoughts like, "You've started so many books that you haven't finished, are you really starting another?" Or "Goals never work for you anyway. They all fail, so why do you bother?" The battle is also bolstered by the unhelpful whining of the inner critic, which, unfortunately, is sometimes co-signed by the voices around us that we expected to help us fight back.

All of this, in combination with the many distractions in life, ultimately keeps us from taking action and seeing the finish line. So, what is the secret to winning this battle? Perspective. Specifically, a winning perspective that gives you an edge on overcoming the aforementioned hurdles and more. In this section, we take a look at the four principles of a winning perspective: Connectedness, Focus, Influence, and Action.

CHAPTER ONE

The Four Areas of Life

"Most of life's battles are won or lost in the mind."
— **Craig Groeschel,** *Soul Detox*

Everyone lives with one of the two following fundamental perspectives. Occasionally, we might sway between the two, but everyone has a clear leaning to one or the other. You can discover which of the two you lean toward by assessing the quality of your decision-making, which is the greatest indicator of your preference between the two perspectives.

The first perspective sees life as generally disconnected. This means living as if actions taken today will have little to no impact on life tomorrow, or worse, failing to see that actions in one area of life could have lasting consequences in others. This perspective usually leads to being surprised by the impact that yesterday's actions and decisions have on today's experience.

A prime example of this is the individual who is unfaithful to their budget but is still surprised when they are financially handicapped by the end of each month. They fail to make the connection between their action (overspending) and the consequences. In this individual's mind, actions and consequences are mutually exclusive.

ALL OF LIFE IS CONNECTED. YOU HAVE THE POWER TO START WRITING YOUR TOMORROWS, TODAY.

The second perspective sees all of life as connected... very connected. It recognizes that a person cannot truly reach goals in one area of life in total isolation from the rest of life. Subsequently, this perspective encourages a far more intentional approach to life and personal growth—a winning perspective.

A great example of this is seen in those who meal prep. They recognize that the demands of their relationships and the fullness of their schedule will not allow them to remain disciplined during the week. So in order to enjoy their relationships and honor their busy schedule while reaching their goal of maintaining a certain diet, they plan and prepare ahead. It's all connected.

This kind of intentionality is vital if you want to not just reach a goal, but to be the kind of person who can reach any goal you set. The good news is that, regardless of the perspective you've had up to this point, you can teach yourself the winning perspective and begin to change your life for the better. This process starts by understanding the four areas of life.

THE FOUR AREAS OF LIFE

Grasping the connectedness of life begins with identifying and understanding its different pieces. There are four areas of life, and within each of these areas there are relationships, responsibilities, and desires that, together, shape us and our lifestyles. Clarity regarding the four areas is a powerful catalyst in forming a winning perspective.

The first area is your **personal life.** This area of life includes anything that has to do with you alone on a personal level. For example, your physical health, spiritual growth, and intellectual development would fall in this area. While you may interact with others when engaged in these things, they are fundamentally your responsibility and no one else's.

The second area is your **family life.** This area includes any familial relationships and responsibilities. We all carry roles in the categories of parent, spouse, sibling, child, etc. Each of these requires something of us in relation to an immediate or extended relative.

The third area is your **social life.** This area includes friendships, mentorships, volunteer work, and other social circles that aren't career- or family-related. Personally, I've also found social life to be one of the hardest areas to plan for.

The fourth and final area is your **career life,** which reflects life at work. If you're a student, this is where you include your *academic career* aspirations. Depending on your age and stage of life, this can secretly become one of the most demanding areas in your life without your realizing it. The same may be true for your social life as well.

The winning perspective depends on being able to see each of these areas clearly as you plan and make decisions. Honoring their connectedness up front can save you from having to repair potential damage from living in their disconnect.

SEEING THE CONNECTEDNESS

In boxing, they say the punch that knocks you out is the one you don't see coming. This is true in life as well, especially in pursuing your goals. For example, have you ever set a goal like losing twenty pounds, only to watch how the rest of your life immediately becomes an obstacle to that goal?

Your work schedule suddenly leaves no extra time for gym appointments, there's a noticeable spike in coffee dates and dinner party invitations, and your mom spontaneously decides to leave you a container of your favorite homemade meal. It is almost as if those other areas of your life never existed before that goal lodged itself into your mind and your heart.

The truth is, as you probably already guessed, those other areas of life were always there, you just didn't see their connectedness. As previously mentioned, seeing all of life as connected is about keeping all four areas in mind as you make decisions and take action. This is especially important as you consider what you want for your future through the goals you set for yourself.

Being mindful of the four areas as you set your goals will allow you to anticipate potential obstacles before you even begin your journey. By doing this, you give your brain a heads-up on what's coming and on how to best prepare for it. In other words, with a connected perspective, you can learn to anticipate many of life's punches.

WHEN LIFE IS DISCONNECTED

Losing balance is often a direct result of a disconnected perspective on life. The disconnectedness causes us to lose track of one or more of the four life areas, and this oversight is what allows the overlooked areas to build up potential deficiencies until they hit a point of crisis. Losing balance happens easily, and, when it does, it is hard to repair.

A young mom who becomes hyper-focused on her family life,

LOSING BALANCE HAPPENS EASILY AND IT IS HARD TO REPAIR WHEN YOU DO.

for example, can easily lose track of her personal life or social life by repeatedly sacrificing her personal time for the sake of the family. Over time, this could lead to severe issues with her physical and mental health.

What's worse is what happens if this imbalance goes unnoticed for too long. Eventually, this mom could hit a point of crisis in one of the overlooked areas of her life. The crisis would force her to halt progress in the areas she is passionate about in order to bring the overlooked area back to a point of health. This is a lesson I learned the hard way.

WHEN I LOST BALANCE

December 2017 was the first time I experienced a serious crisis as a result of a disconnected perspective in life. The January before, I had accepted the position of Student Ministry Pastor at my home church, and I was elated. I would be doing something I loved and was passionate about with people I loved. My time in this position is something I would not trade for the world, and it taught me many things, including what I am about to share with you.

I came into the position knowing that there was much work to do in the student ministry department, and I had a robust plan to match the demand. Wasting no time, I hit the ground running, working meticulously the entire year through my three-phase plan of establishing a healthy foundation for ministry to young adults and teens. I invested countless hours in restructuring my team, our goals, our culture, and our partnership with local schools.

In between meeting with mentors, students, leaders, and parents, I committed to preparing a weekly message, sometimes more on special occasions. While all of this activity was prefaced with and born from prayer, there was still a fundamental flaw in my work—I lost track of my personal and family life in different ways.

By the time December arrived, I was exhausted but too busy to notice. My body, however, did not overlook my poor self-care. Additionally, I was emotionally drained as a result of spending very little time with my family, which usually refills me. My highly awaited weeklong Christmas break was riddled with anxiety, exhaustion, and bouts of depression that I had never experienced before. Something had to change, and I knew I had to be the one to change it.

> FOR MOST OF US THE PROBLEM ISN'T THAT WE AIM TOO HIGH AND FAIL. IT'S JUST THE OPPOSITE: WE AIM TOO LOW AND SUCCEED.
> - SIR. KEN ROBINSON

I still loved what I did, and my position allowed me flexibility in managing my schedule, so I knew immediately that the change I needed was internal. Much of what you will read in the remainder of this book is a direct result of the journey that ensued following that alarming Christmas break. Like I'm recommending to you, my journey started with returning to the connectedness of life.

EXERCISE: SEEING THE CONNECTION

Here are a few exercises to help you bring the four areas of your life into focus so you can see their connectedness. Use the companion workbook mentioned in the introduction to complete these and the other exercises not listed in this book. Completing the exercises will set you up for the next chapter.

1. List your six most significant responsibilities for each area of life. Doing this will help you bring maximum clarity to your life's connectedness. This is not only helpful for seeing with clarity, but it's also very helpful for goal-setting.

2. In a separate list, identify the three most significant people in each area of your life. A part of seeing life as connected is recognizing that there are always key people attached to your goals. I call them *priority people*. For example, if your goal is to lose weight but your wife does all the cooking, then it would be foolish to overlook her.

3. If you haven't created any goals yet, dream big and write four goals for each area of life. Sometimes just seeing everything clearly, helps to reveal where changes are most needed in your life. Be brutally honest and dare to dream big.

Bonus: Power Goals. A power goal is a goal that has an

impact across multiple areas of life. For example, introducing daily exercise to your life can improve your health, give you more energy for time with your family, and potentially improve your productivity at work. Aiming for Power Goals will set you up to go further faster.

4. If you've already created a set of goals, assign each goal to the area of life it's associated with. Are all of your goals in one or two areas of life? Considering your other responsibilities, are your goals realistic for your schedule or current season of life? Be brutally honest.

While this list isn't exhaustive, it will help you to bring clarity to the connectedness of your life without overwhelming you. Take your time to work through this exercise and those in the workbook, and think through each area of life thoroughly. Once you've completed this, start the next chapter.

CHAPTER TWO

No Focus, No Power

"The easiest way to kill a person's dream is to give them another one."
— Anonymous

If your goals were a train heading to a brighter future, then a lack of focus would be the brick wall built over the tracks. It's not an understatement to say that focus is a vital part of moving us to action. Without focus, it is possible to be moving but never make progress.

Have you ever wondered why a lion tamer uses a chair to enter the cage of a man-eating beast? Seriously, of all the tools in the world, a chair is the best he can do? Yes, actually, and it's genius! See, as the tamer points the four legs of the chair toward the lion, it tries to focus on all four legs at once. The inability to focus renders this powerful and ferocious beast paralyzed. The lion is unable to move, simply because its brain is unable to lock in on one target.[1] How's your focus?

THE BADGE OF BUSY

Neurologists have discovered that our brains aren't much different from the lion's in this regard. When we dilute our focus, spreading it thinly across many tasks, responsibilities, and goals, we render ourselves ineffective. So yes, you may have the power and intelligence to launch the next Fortune 500 company, scale Mount Everest, or reclaim your physical health, but if you're focusing on too many things at once, you might be giving that power away.

What's crazier is that we easily trick ourselves into diluting our focus because it feels good. It feels great, actually. Think about how many people have confidently and proudly told you how busy they are in the last seven days alone. It seems that being busy has become synonymous with being productive in the eyes of our society, and this is not only untrue, it's also not good.

I'll admit that I also fell for this culturally imposed *stay-busy* philosophy before learning better. For me, the shift started as far back as high school but solidified itself into my perspective during college. I can first recall feeling a strong sense of guilt when I wasn't doing something "productive" as a student in college. This led me to almost always keep my planner full.

I also saw signs of the negative impact of this philosophy on my life during my years as a full-time musician. Independent artists naturally wear multiple hats when launching their careers, much like entrepreneurs. Young artists often have to be their own managers, promoters, producers, and much more. This reality, for me, compounded with the stay-busy philosophy, creating a dangerous whirlwind of constant activity.

"GOOD IS THE ENEMY OF GREAT."

- JIM COLLINS, GOOD TO GREAT[3]

I would shift from trying to book shows to working on an unfinished song, then promoting content to small radio stations or securing interview slots, all while managing multiple social media platforms to grow engagement and awareness. The biggest problem with spreading my focus so thin was that inspiration mostly finds me in my downtime when I am relaxed. My activity whirlwind was a setup for failure on multiple levels.

After taking a serious financial, mental, and emotional hit through a scam that cost my wife and me nearly twelve thousand dollars, I was forced to stop. I knew that if I was going to succeed long-term in the career I had chosen, I would need help. In a desperate attempt not to give up after taking such a loss, knowing that I simply would not be able to bounce back if I stopped there, I shifted my focus to building a team around me.

Through a contact at Sony-RED, I was introduced to Billy

Holland of The Holland Group, which is an artist management, brand development, and label-facilitation company based in Nashville, Tennessee. After a few conversations, Billy agreed to take me on as an artist and work with me to build my brand. Billy and his amazing team coached me through a more focused and strategic approach to artist development, brand strategy as an artist, and eventually starting my own independent record label.

My biggest lesson when I started to work with The Holland Group was learning to do less. I quickly discovered that it takes discipline to go against the grain of our hustle culture, to be okay with keeping only a few things on my plate because those few things are a big deal. In other words, it takes more discipline to do less.

Warren Buffett underscored this when he famously said, "... really successful people say no to almost everything!"[2] In this statement, Buffett was pointing out that really successful people understood the power of focus and thus preferred to do a few things well instead of diluting their efforts.

So how do you narrow your focus? Good question! There are three main ways to do it.

1.   Say No More Often

2.   Limit Draining Information

3.   Filter Your Goals

SAY NO MORE OFTEN

In his best-selling book *Good To Great*, Jim Collins explores the idea that the enemy of greatness and excellence is mediocrity. "Good enough" is the greatest roadblock to *great*. Another way of understanding this is that when we fill our calendars by saying "yes" to every *good* opportunity that comes our way, we dilute our chances of maximizing the few *great* opportunities that will come.

1. Count The Cost. Every time you say yes to an opportunity, you are automatically saying no to another. Counting the cost is all about making sure that it's worth it. For example, is working late one more night worth missing dinner with your family, *again*?

2. Start With "No." For those who are bold, I recommend making your default answer to new requests a strong "no" without being a jerk about it. Practicing saying "no" more often forces us to be intentional with where we choose to invest our time, resources, and energy. If you find it difficult to say "no" sometimes, keep in mind that a simple and polite offer to reschedule is often sufficient. You can say something like, "This isn't a good time for me, can we reschedule for a few weeks from now?"

LIMIT DRAINING INFORMATION

The information we consume either drains us or fuels us. This is completely subject to your wiring. The goal is to limit as much of the draining information intake as possible because when we are drained, we become poor decision makers.

The reality is that this isn't entirely within your control. For things like work and some family updates, you just have to be present and navigate the situation as it comes. On the other hand, things like the news and most of our social media are largely unnecessary and draining.

TRYING TO REACH GOALS THAT YOU'RE NOT TRULY INTERESTED IN IS AN INVESTMENT IN LONG-TERM FAILURE.

1. Limit Social Media. Spending hours on social media looking at things you wish you had or subconsciously comparing yourself to others is draining. It steals the energy you'll need when it's time to take action on your goals.

2. Limit Bad News. Stay informed but limit or eliminate unnecessary bad news, gossip, or anything like it. Doing this helps you naturally develop a more positive and winning perspective on life and your future. Developing this kind of outlook makes taking action easier when the time comes.

FILTER YOUR GOALS

An important part of narrowing your focus is filtering your goals. The aim here is to separate the goals that are just the result of social pressure from those that are truly meaningful to you. Identify the ones with roots that are deeper than people's opinions.

Never set your goals from a place of jealousy, for example. Trying to reach goals that you're not truly interested in is an investment in long-term failure. Set goals from a place of clarity, as we explored in the previous chapter.

Moving forward, I want you to start thinking about goal-setting as a skill and not a responsibility, meaning, it's something that you can get better at over time and with practice. They don't currently teach this in school, or at home for that matter, because most people don't see it this way.

If your goal is anything less than a genuine reflection of the future that you want for yourself or the people around you, the motivation to push through when things get tough will be non-existent. If you didn't do the exercise at the end of Chapter One to get that clarity, go back and do it before moving on.

EXERCISE: THE FUNNEL FILTER

Here's a great way to filter your goals. As you do this, be honest with yourself about which of the goals are truly meaningful to you on a deep level. This is an exercise from Warren Buffett[3] that I've modified:

1. From the sixteen goals that you set in Chapter One, identify the top eight goals that are most important. Be sure to consider the four areas and *keep at least one goal from each area.*

You can use your workbook to complete this exercise.

2. Next, from the remaining eight, identify your top four goals from that list. Select one goal for each area of life. This will be important for the remainder of the book. When you're finished, draw a line through every goal that did not make your top four. Keep in mind that those goals aren't gone forever, but that reaching the ones in front of you now will empower you to reach the other ones faster when it's time.

3. Finally, write down your selected four goals somewhere you will be able to see them daily. The point of this is to narrow your focus and target your energy completely toward these top four goals alone for now. If done right, you'll most likely reach these goals much more quickly than anticipated because of the focused energy toward them.

In your workbook, write these goals in your dashboard where you can view them regularly.

Unhealthy
Relationships
Don't Often
Lead To A
Healthy You.

CHAPTER THREE

Synchronizing Brainwaves

"You see how picky I am about my shoes, and they only go on my feet."
— **Cher, Clueless**

Andy Stanley, an author, pastor, and speaker, teaches that our friends help to determine the direction and quality of our lives.[1] A simple observation helps to make that very clear; however, few people act on this knowledge. For the sake of your future, you have to challenge this reality and choose to be in that few.

The voices you allow to speak into your journey are vital, and sometimes fatal, when it comes to developing a winning perspective. You already have a clear inner critic ruthlessly picking at your goals from the start, so be relentless in guarding yourself against the *outer* ones. Pessimistic friends can have the best intentions and the worst impact, both at the same time.

Now, let's be clear. I'm not suggesting you drop all of your friends, although if you have horrible ones, it's 100% worth it. What I am suggesting is that you be extra picky about who you talk to about your goals and your journey toward them.

BECOMING AN AUTHOR

My journey to becoming an author was one of my most guarded goals. Altogether, only about six or seven people in total, between family and close friends, knew about my goal to write. Even fewer knew I was working on this book until the first draft was completed. Actually, I think only my wife was aware.

> "BEING PICKY ABOUT YOUR INNER CIRCLE ISN'T PRIDEFUL. IT'S WISDOM. JESUS HAD TWELVE DISCIPLES BUT HIS INNER CIRCLE WAS ONLY THREE."

Choosing not to share wasn't a matter of trustworthiness as much as it was a result of self-awareness. I knew how important and how fragile the goal of finishing this book was to me, and I was determined to guard that. I also learned over time that even great friends with good intentions can have a negative impact, especially if they know too much too soon.

On the other hand, a healthy friend may help you reach your

goals faster. One such friend for me is Joey, who I've known for more than ten years now. Joey and I share a background in music, as well as in ministry, and our shared experiences have helped us learn how to best help each other. Over the years, we've developed a unique relationship that allows us to encourage each other's goals while simultaneously still being able to challenge and assist one another in refining them when necessary.

Learning to guard your goals is a simple way of making sure your inner critic doesn't have any reinforcement from the outside before you can develop what you need internally to get to the finish line. For me, after I finished this book's first draft I knew I had all I needed to fight back any internal or external thoughts that would threaten the book's completion.

SELECTIVE SYNCING

Have you ever felt like you have an almost telepathic connection with your spouse, sibling, or best friend? Have you felt that somehow they are able to know what you are thinking or what you're about to say before you even say it? Well, there is more to it than you think.

The relationship between Danny Ocean and Rusty in the *Ocean's* movie trilogy[2], directed by Steven Soderbergh, is one of my favorite cinematic friendships that exemplifies this kind of connection. In each movie, you can find Danny, played by George

Clooney, and Rusty, played by Brad Pitt, having their classic conversations composed of incomplete sentences. These scenes are thoroughly entertaining and a clear example of two brains in sync. Even my wife and I aren't quite on their level yet.

One of my favorite scenes from the trilogy that exemplifies this idea takes place in *Ocean's Thirteen*[3], which finds Danny and Rusty walking next to the Bellagio Fountain while discussing relationships.

Rusty vents, "Relationships can be…"

"Sure," Danny cuts him off in response.

Rusty continues, "But they're also…"

"That's right," Danny chimes in before Rusty can finish. They stroll on before changing the subject of the conversation. While this is an entertaining example, there is much more happening here.

According to research from The Basque Center on Cognition, Brain and Language (BCBL), "The rhythms of brainwaves between two people taking part in a conversation begin to match each other."[4] How amazing is that? Our brains sync up with the people we talk to the longest and most often. This neurological function is the reason your spouse or best friend is able to *just know* what you are thinking at times without you uttering a single word, similar to Danny and Rusty in the scene from *Ocean's Thirteen*.

Neuroscientist Moran Cerf used similar research[5] to determine that when trying to develop new habits, the most important decision we can make is who we surround ourselves with. If you want to start eating healthier, for example, find people who are already eating healthy and avoid eating with those who do not. It's not selfish, it's science.

WHO TO PICK?

Selective syncing also has a significant impact on how we deal with things like change, stress, anxiety, and much more, but that's for another book. In the meantime, here are a few questions to help you determine if you should talk to a given person about your goals:

1. Is their default disposition positive or negative? A default disposition is a perspective or attitude someone carries the majority of the time. Now, the reality is that everyone has bad days. No one is truly positive and happy all the time, but everyone has a default disposition.

The people you allow to speak into your goals when they're most fragile should be the people who will speak life into them, not the ones who will end up co-signing your inner critic.

2. Do they have a habit of making good decisions? Don't overthink this one. It's often very clear if someone is a chronically poor decision-maker. Sometimes our sympathy can try to justify their victimhood, but do your best to just look at the facts.

Remember, having a habit of poor decision-making does not make someone a bad person. They just make poor decisions.

Separating these two ideas will make the filtering process easier for you.

> WHEN TRYING TO DEVELOP NEW HABITS, THE MOST IMPORTANT DECISION WE CAN MAKE IS WHO WE SURROUND OURSELVES WITH.

Someone who has a habit of making bad decisions concerning their own life will most likely be okay with the same reality for you too. Additionally, if your goal is centered on making a good decision (or a series of good decisions) for yourself, your future, or your family, they aren't the ones to help you get to that goal.

3. Do they keep it real with you? This is vitally important. The people who truly care about your future are the ones who become genuinely upset with you when *you* make a bad decision concerning *your* future. Friends like these are keepers for life, and vital on your journey.

If they recognize your goal as truly beneficial to you, your future, or your family, they will become your greatest advocates. They will encourage you when you need it, and in the way that you may need to hear it.

4. Do they know how to be serious? Friends who aren't able to be serious about truly serious things are dangerous in general and very dangerous to your goals. Keep in mind that if everything is a joke to them, then that would include your future, your health, and possibly you yourself. I don't take things like that lightly and you shouldn't either.

Just a note on this: It's often hard to determine a funny friend's default because they're so fun to talk to. However, you should not skip this step for anyone. When it comes to having serious conversations, what's their default? Funny or not, find it. These friends may be great to hang with, but they're likely not the best ones to build with. Assess them well before choosing to allow them to speak into your goals.

EXERCISE: SETTING BOUNDARIES

What happens if there is someone negative in your circle that you can't keep your goal from? I've spoken to many, for example, who share that their parents or spouse are their biggest critics. They feel that their loved ones are always putting them down whenever they're trying something new.

If you find yourself in this situation, I recommend setting some verbal boundaries. As Brené Brown said, "Clear is kind. Unclear is unkind."[6] Meaning, when you clearly explain what you expect of someone, it's an act of kindness that allows them to act accordingly.

Use these questions to identify potential boundaries you may need to establish as you begin your journey:

1. **Are they allowed to ask about your progress?**

2. **Do you need anything from them to complete your goal? If so, what is it, how often, and when?**

3. **Are they allowed to comment on your goal or progress?**

4. **What are they explicitly not allowed to say or do regarding your goal?**

5. **Are they willing to sign a written contract that clearly states these and other conditions?**

If someone is clearly belligerent and unreasonable concerning your boundaries in this regard, then remove yourself from the environment as often as possible, even if it means walking around with headphones on for a few months just to drown them out. Do not let them discourage you from starting or finishing your journey. If the individual is your spouse, try finding a third party to help with communicating, maybe a counselor, so that the pursuit of your goals does not become the end of your marriage.

Use your workbook to filter your circle of friends and family through these questions and others. This will help you to determine who is truly capable of being an ally with you on this journey and who you may need to love from a distance.

CHAPTER FOUR

Preparing for Action

"Action is the foundational key to all success."
— **Pablo Picasso**

While the principles I've shared so far are powerful, they're not magical. The final step in winning the mental battle and guaranteeing your victory is to take action. Showing up and doing the work is your most important step. People learn this and immediately become intimidated, because this is exactly where they so often fail themselves.

They create the plan and buy the gear needed to reach their goals, then fail to show up when it's time to take action. This lack of showing up often leaves them in a serious pity party, beating themselves up.

Don't be afraid. The "failure to show up" syndrome, as I call it, is not an unbreakable cycle. As a matter of fact, this chapter and the next section are all about how to break that cycle and start taking action more consistently than ever before.

There are two notable reasons why you should be determined to take action when it comes to your goals. The first is that it is the final and biggest step in silencing your inner critic. The second reason is that your goals only exist on the other side of action, and nowhere else!

SILENCING YOUR INNER CRITIC

Taking action is the most significant step in silencing your inner critic. Often misunderstood, your inner critic is not your enemy. It's more like your emotional security guard, except it's only as brave as Scooby-Doo and Shaggy, if you know what I mean.

When your inner critic begins to nag you, it is often just trying to protect you from a negative emotion because that's its job. It doesn't want you to feel pain, failure, rejection, etc., and it will do everything it can to keep you from taking action if it senses even the possibility of these things.[1]

You can only prove to your inner critic that the action is not so bad after taking the risk and proving that you are still safe. This is why, when we are trying to build up the confidence to do something scary, we say things like, "I've gone through worse and survived" or "What's the worst that can happen? After all, I *did* (fill in the blank) before." In short, we are reminding ourselves that safety is on the other side of the experience.

> "ACT AS IF WHAT YOU DO MAKES A DIFFERENCE. IT DOES."
>
> - WILLIAM JAMES, PHILOSOPHER [3]

However, there is a way to take action that allows your inner critic to be less afraid as well as build confidence during the process, a path with less internal resistance to showing up when it's time. We will look more deeply into this idea in Chapters Five and Six.

THE OTHER SIDE OF ACTION

The second important reason to take action is that your goals only exist on the other side of action. Your journey toward your goals will be clearer and more enjoyable the moment you embrace this reality and make it a regular part of how you think. Progress is on the other side of the steps you take.

The couch potato who wants to win a marathon only has a chance if he starts running. The office worker who wants to be an author can only get published if she starts to write. The list goes on and on, but I think you get it. Your goals only exist on the other side of action.

Picture your goal as a prisoner behind the bars of inaction. The problem is that we often view these bars as unbreakable. We convince ourselves that it is not even worth trying to overcome them. Your goals want to get out and, more importantly, you want them out! But if you never begin to take action, they will remain imprisoned. Taking action weakens and eventually completely destroys the bars that imprison your goals.

THE DOWNSIDE OF IDEATION

Generally at about this point people find themselves saying something like, "I just don't think you understand, Paul. This is really a big struggle for me and has been the demise of many of my goals." To which I respond, "Trust me, if anyone understands how significant of a hurdle this is, it's me."

For more than a year and a half, I had a weekly breakfast meeting with Joey, my friend who I mentioned in the last chapter, and where we discussed everything that life sent our way during these meetings. Our conversations included religion, work, goals, marriage, parenting, and anything else that came up. Being creatives, we often talked about new ideas and projects we were working on or thinking about.

During one of our regular meetings, I received a much-needed wake up call. That morning, after getting my tea, I found Joey in our usual seating area at our local Starbucks. We exchanged greetings as I sat across from him and began to catch up. I was excited about a new idea I had for a planner and we eventually got to talking about it, when the conversation took an unusual turn.

"That's a great idea!" Joey remarked, and then continued, "What's your next step with it? When does it launch?"

"Actually, I'm not sure," I said. "It's not really where I want it to be yet. I'm still tweaking it."

Joey paused for a while before responding, "Paul, this is a great idea, but I've gotta say I'm a little afraid for it."

I was confused. "*Afraid* for it? What do you mean?" I asked.

"Good ideas tend to die with you, man. You think and process them to death."

I was stunned silent and in disbelief at the truth bomb that my friend had so casually delivered. It was as if he held up a mirror and allowed me to see a character defect in myself that I had never seen before. It stung, but in a healthy way.

His observation was later underscored in a personality strengths assessment that I took for work called the CliftonStrengths Assessment[2]. In it, I discovered that one of my top five personality strengths is ideation, which simply means I'm fascinated and inspired by new ideas and can easily think them up. The downside to the ideation strength, unfortunately, is that I can easily get stuck on the idea and *lack follow-through*[3], which was my problem.

While I wasn't thrilled with this new discovery about myself, it motivated me. I saw it as a new opportunity to grow. Needless to say, Joey and I spent the rest of our conversation dissecting this truth bomb and helping me to map my way out of it. The greatest lesson I've learned from that journey so far is that taking actions, even small imperfect ones, is always more powerful than a great idea that is never acted on.

EXERCISE: WHAT'S AT STAKE

A key component to taking action when it is hardest is knowing what is really at stake if you don't. This can be a deeply compelling way to keep going when you start to lose steam. Answer the questions below to help you identify what's at stake when it comes to taking action.

1. What could you lose? Our goals can sometimes seem trivial in the midst of our busy lives until we stop to really think about them. For example, why do you want to get healthy? Is it really because you want a beach body? Maybe it's because you want to live long enough and be healthy enough to enjoy your potential grandkids?

Sometimes when we consider the implications of not designing a healthier lifestyle, we can see scary futures. We can envision futures where our inaction causes us to fail our marriages, squander our kids' futures, compromise our financial security, or even destroy our health. What could you lose if you don't reach your goal?

2. What could you gain? The potential benefits of success are sometimes just as motivating as the potential damage of inaction. For example, what could you gain if you did finish that book? Or if you *did* develop those healthy habits you've wanted for so long?

In the same way that we looked at the extreme of our potential losses, I want you to dream big on the gains. Could your new healthy habits lead to you pull your family out of poverty and start that dream business? Could your novel be the next New York Times Best Seller that gets turned into a series of blockbusters? I think so!

> *TAKING ACTION, EVEN SMALL IMPERFECT ONES, IS ALWAYS MORE POWERFUL THAN A GREAT IDEA THAT IS NEVER ACTED ON.*

3. Who else will benefit from your action? The truth is that you are never the only one affected by your action. There is always someone else on the other side of your action whose life will be impacted for better or worse. Even with something as personal as losing weight, someone in your life will benefit from it.

For example, your new healthier habits not only unravel a better future for you, they're also a great example for your kids. Your goals start with you, but they always include much more than you.

4. What story do you want to tell? You write the story of your life one decision at a time, as famously said by Andy Stanley.[4] What story are you writing? When your kids, grandkids, and potentially others talk about your life, there *will* be something to talk about. But what will it be?

A story worth telling is written by people who take intentional action toward intimidating goals. The ones who decided the reward is worth the risk. On the other hand, doing nothing is a great way to ensure that your story is a story that the future will try to avoid bringing up.

Take your time thinking through these questions and capturing your response in your workbook. You'll want to be able to revisit these answers along your journey.

Part Two

A Better Way To Take Action

PART TWO OVERVIEW

A BETTER WAY TO TAKE ACTION

In this section, we step out of the psychology of goal-setting and begin to outline a strategic way of taking action toward your goals. As previously mentioned, your goals only exist on the other side of action; however, taking action consistently can be difficult for many. They get to this part of their journey, ready to take on the mountain, only to find that their method of taking action is itself an obstacle.

Traditional methods of taking action toward our goals often fail to consider our psychological wiring, which directly correlates to how we interact with the physical world. This means that no matter how great our method, techniques, or routines are, if they don't take into consideration how our brains naturally function they themselves will become obstacles. In other words, our approach to taking action can become the very thing that keeps us from taking action consistently.

The four principles discussed in this section of the book will empower you to take action in a way that honors the way our brains are naturally wired, regardless of your personality. They are foundationally aligned with how our brains have come to navigate the world and how we naturally form new habits. Using these principles, you will find that taking action consistently will become easier and the path to your goals will become clearer.

CHAPTER FIVE

Stop Planning!

"You can't use an old map to explore a new world."
— **Albert Einstein**

From this point on I want you to view your goals not as things you want to do, but as places you want to go. They are the destinations you are working toward in the different areas of your life. This is an important distinction to make as you begin to take action toward your goals.

Picking up the mail after work, for example, is something you *do*. Living a healthier life (losing twenty pounds and keeping it off, for example), is a *destination* you move toward. The former is something you do and then forget, never really having to think of it again. The latter is a new way of living that requires new habits, new perspectives, and potentially new people around you. They are not the same by any measure.

Think of it this way: if you're trying to get things done, then you need a plan, but if you want to get to new places, then what you need is a map. This simple distinction is at the heart of why most *plans* fail when it comes to reaching goals. There are a lot of great definitions of a map, but I love how dictionary.cambridge.org puts it: *"a... drawing that shows a direction of travel between one place and another."*[1]

In other words, a map shows you where one thing is in relation to another. Mapping your way to your goals means getting clarity on where you are, where you want to go, and how to best get there. Seeing and approaching your goals in this way reveals the significance of every step you take, even the small steps.

If you are unable to see the relationship between where you are and where you want to go, you are effectively lost and it will show. Beyond that, when we are unable to see if we are making progress in the right direction, every step becomes more difficult to take. Using a map makes taking action toward your goals easier to do.

COMPONENTS OF A MAP

Almost every map has the following fundamental components:

a symbol that identifies true north, a terrain description to help determine things like elevation, rivers, and other unique elements you may come across, and finally, a scale to help measure distance —this is essential.

1. The True North. The true north symbol is vital on every map because it's the only thing that gives direction to your journey and keeps you from getting lost. On your life map, true north is your philosophical anchor that gives meaning to your goals beyond the surface. This is why we spent time answering the question, "What's *really* at stake when it comes to your goals?" You defined the true north for that goal through your answers.

> "LIFE IS WHAT HAPPENS TO US WHILE WE ARE MAKING OTHER PLANS."
> - ALLEN SAUNDERS[3]

For example, this year's goal for the "career" area of my life is to lead my business passionately and grow its profit to replace or exceed my previous annual income. On the surface, it can sound like I just want to have a big business. However, my true north is that as a husband and hopefully a future father, I believe God made it my responsibility to care and provide for my family, and I'm determined to do that well.

With this perspective in mind, I always have clarity about what's really at stake for me. Having such compelling elements as my true north helps me to bounce back from serious losses, lift my head, dig my heels in, and get back to work. It is possible to have one *true north* that drives many goals or a different *true north* for each of your goals. Neither approach is wrong.

2. The Terrain Description. The terrain description on a map helps prepare you for what to expect on your journey. It tells you at what point you will have smooth roads, deep valleys, or intimidating mountains. This information tells you how to prepare to be successful on your journey.

On your life map, life experience is the best descriptor of upcoming terrain. Here's what I mean: If you've tried to reach any of your current goals before (or tried to reach past goals that are similar to your current goals), take time to reflect on what the journey was like. What was most difficult about it, and what was easiest? What will you need to do differently this time around? These moments of intentional reflection can sometimes be enough to shifts the odds in your favor.

Another way of determining the terrain between you and your goals is through the life experience of others, through finding a coach or mentor or through reading and research. Most of the places we are trying to get to in life carry the footprints of people who have walked the path before, and often those trailblazers are willing to give you a heads-up on what to expect. Look for blog posts, YouTube videos, books, and other mediums where people may have shared their experiences. Chances are, there are plenty of them to learn from.

When my wife and I started our first business, an independent record label with a major distribution deal, we had no prior business ownership experience, especially in the music industry. We buried ourselves in books on the topic and eventually found mentors. Don't be afraid to learn from other people's experiences and mistakes so you can avoid repeating them.

3. The Distance Scale. Finally, the scale on a map is designed to help you to see how close or how far you are from your intended destination. On your life map, a clearly defined and measurable goal is your distance scale. As we already discussed, goal-setting is a skill you can improve, and this is one way to do that.

Revisit the goals you set in the first section of this book. Are they measurable or lofty? A lofty goal will drain you, run you in circles, and then leave you hanging with nothing to show for it. A measurable goal lets you know exactly when you've hit the mark or how much longer you have to go in order to achieve it.

Here are a few examples of lofty versus measurable goals:

Lofty:

☐ I want to lose some weight so I can feel more energetic.

☐ I want to run my own business and make a lot of money.

Measurable:

☐ I want to lose twenty-five pounds and exercise daily.

☐ I want to own my own business and earn an annual take-home income of $x from it.

A great measurable goal makes success exceptionally tangible. Review each of your goals and use the designated area in your workbook to write out clearly defined and measurable goals.

VIDA MAP

After years of searching for the right tool to help me on my own journey, it became clear that it didn't exist. So I created one. I will admit, however, that when I began to design this tool I thought I was designing a planner, a customized planner that would reflect my current season of life, as well as highlight and manage my priorities. Among other things, work-life balance was a primary filter during the design process.

> A MEASURABLE GOAL MAKES SUCCESS EXCEPTIONALLY TANGIBLE.

In using it, however, I found that this "planner" made taking action toward my goals much easier for me. I was able to see clearly how the small steps that I took daily were connected to my larger long-term goals. No step was too small or insignificant, which in turn made me more consistent in taking action.

After completing the early versions and using it myself, I introduced the idea to my friends and colleagues as a planner. Over time, after explaining its many functions repeatedly to others, it became clear to me that what I was describing was not a traditional planner, but instead, a functional life map, a life map that helps to track my goals and priorities, manage my life balance, and narrow my focus. I call it VIDA map; *Vida* is translated as "life" in many European languages.

I call it a map because it helps to do all the things I described above. VIDA map coaches you through clearly defining your goals, identifying your true north, and assessing the terrain between where you are and your goal destination. It includes the functionality of an annual, monthly, weekly, and daily planner. As a bonus element to this book, I've made a free downloadable version available for you as a reader at www.paulwcroswell.com/LifeBalanceResources. Visit this link to claim your VIDA map.

CHAPTER SIX

Big Goals... Small Steps

"A journey of a thousand miles begins with a single step."

— Lao Tzu

This may sound cliché and even overdone, but a small step in the right direction is a big deal. If you've struggled with improving in any area of your life, this principle may be your missing link. As we look further into taking action toward your goals, it is vital that you are equipped with this perspective.

I talk often about this idea of small steps on my blog. It's also the basis for my podcast, *The Pocket Potential,* because it's been so transformative in my own life and successes. The practice of taking small steps is also a big part of how I wrote this book and finished the first draft in just over a week. I share more on that later.

The small steps idea was first introduced to me by Steven Guise through his international bestseller *Mini Habits*[1]. Applying the idea helped to completely shift my lifestyle and eliminated almost all negative self-talk related to reaching my goals. It's what I like to call a common-sense idea (that just isn't very common).

In this chapter, I'll give you the *Mini Habits* for dummies breakdown, explaining the fundamentals to help you understand the power of mini-habits and how to apply them. If you are interested in going even deeper, I highly recommend Guise's book for a more thorough understanding of mini-habits.

A SMALL STEP IN THE RIGHT DIRECTION IS A BIG DEAL!

SMALL... NO, SMALLER!

An important thing to note on this topic is that when I say "small," I mean laughably small. Seriously, if you do this right, friends and family who know what you are doing will probably laugh. For example, if your goal is to run a half-marathon, a laughably small step may be that you park further away from entrances in parking lots so that you start walking more. It's laughable to some, but it works.

The goal is to make the first step so easy that it would be

almost crazy for you *not* to do it. The key here is recognizing that it's the *first* step. You start there, but you don't stay there. As mentioned earlier, I personally subscribe to this practice and still build it into my daily life.

When I decided to write this book, it felt daunting. I had tried writing books before and that clearly didn't work out for me, as many of them are still just incomplete manuscripts. When starting this book, I knew the content I wanted to share, and I knew I needed a strategy for documenting that content, but that was pretty much the extent of my plan.

Eventually, I remembered the mini-habit strategy and decided to apply it. I set my mini-habit goal of 500 words per day and started on my journey. To my surprise, at the end of day eight, I had a completed 12,000-word first draft that was cohesive and readable, and that was largely because, once I had momentum from my mini-habit goal, I would almost always write more. This book alone is proof that the principle of this chapter works, but there's more.

THREE REASONS TO TAKE SMALL STEPS

There are three specific reasons why I recommend this idea when it comes to taking action toward your goals. First, small steps make any goal more manageable, regardless of how intimidating the goal may be. Second, successful small steps are investments in personal confidence for reaching future goals. Finally, small steps have a powerful snowball effect that's worth its weight in gold when it comes to making progress.

1. It's Manageable. The most intuitive reason for breaking your goals into laughably small steps is that it makes your goals more manageable. It creates the ability for you to take your daily or weekly action step *almost* without thought and with minimal internal resistance. Your inner critic will have very little to fight against, and it will be even harder to make an excuse for not doing it.

If your small step is one sit-up a day, it will be difficult to make an excuse for not accomplishing it. On the other hand, if your goal was thirty sit-ups a day, it becomes easy to rationalize not even starting. The inner resistance to the two goals is vastly different.

2. It's a Confidence Investment. Whenever you set a goal and reach it, your brain rewards itself with a sense of accomplishment and a dose of dopamine. Dopamine is known as a "feel-good neurotransmitter," a neurochemical that boosts your mood, motivation, attention, and helps to regulate movement, learning, and emotional responses.[2] Your body produces and releases this chemical as a way of rewarding you.

Dopamine is released when you get a notification that excites you, when you're having sex as a way of boosting pleasure, and, yes, when you reach your goals, no matter how big or small they are. So every time I hit or surpassed my goal of 500 words, my body released some dopamine. What's more exciting is that when it was time to write again, I would be less resistant because my brain wanted the dopamine effect. Call it a positive addiction or brain hacking.

This is also why former Navy SEAL Admiral William McRaven recommends that if you want to change your life, then you should start by making your bed every morning[3]. It gives you a sense of accomplishment and your brain begins to look for more of that feeling throughout the day, which brings me to my final reason.

IF YOU WANT TO CHANGE YOUR LIFE, THEN YOU SHOULD START BY MAKING YOUR BED EVERY MORNING.

3. It Has a Snowball Effect. Successfully taking your small steps consistently has a powerful snowball effect. As a result of the regular sense of accomplishment and a healthy daily dose of dopamine, you will find that you want to do more than the small step that you set. This is the snowball effect.

For example, if your small step is to journal three sentences a day, you'll find that after doing that consistently, you naturally desire to write much more than three sentences. I had a similar experience when I started this book. My mini-habit goal or small step was 500 words per day, but naturally, I ended up writing about 800 to 1000 words on average. The same is true for other types of goals as well. If you plan a daily small step of one sit-up a day, you'll naturally *want* to do much more over time.

THE HABIT BUILDING CYCLE

Nir Eyal explains the habit-building cycle as a rotation of trigger, action, reward, and investment[4]. The *trigger* begins externally but over time should become internal. For example, when you first start working out, you may need to set a reminder to "trigger" or tell you when it is time to start your workout or leave for the gym. Over time, the trigger will become internal so that at a certain time of day, you automatically have an internal desire to workout.

The *action* is what we are supposed to, or what we planned to do. The action in this case would be your small step. So when your trigger, or reminder, alerts you, the action you take would be to change and begin your workout or to leave for the gym. We will explore the importance of the trigger and the action in the next chapter.

The *reward* is what you get for faithfully completing the action. The initial reward, as previously mentioned, starts with the dopamine effect and a sense of accomplishment, but an external reward enhances the likelihood of you repeating the cycle. For example, a potential reward after your workout could be having your favorite healthy snack or watching a few episodes of your favorite show. We unpack the significance of strategically celebrating your small wins more in Chapter Nine.

The final part of the cycle is the *investment*. This is the long-term benefit that comes from engaging the entire cycle consistently.

The investment, in this case, is the progress you make toward your goal and ultimately reaching your goal. In other words, the investment would be watching the numbers on the scale get lower and lower until you reach your goal weight.

Approaching your goals with an understanding of the habit-building cycle equips you to achieve lasting change and transformation through them. Your goals become much more than something to accomplish when seen this way; they turn into stepping stones toward a healthier and happier you.

EXERCISE: BREAKING DOWN YOUR GOALS

Now it's time to revisit your goals and begin to break them down into small steps. You can use your workbook or your VIDA map to capture your response. Be sure to do the following exercise with each of your goals. It may feel tedious, but it is an important step in moving forward.

1. If your goal is long-term (meaning it will take more than a year to accomplish), what's one step you can take this year to move toward it?

2. What's one thing you can do this month to move toward this year's target?

3. What's one thing you can do this week to move toward this month's target?

4. What's one thing you can do today to move toward this

week's target?

I shared a personal example of this in the workbook for you to use as a guide. If you've downloaded VIDA map to use on your journey, you'll notice that there's a space for you to do this exercise regularly to keep track of your goals in all the areas of life.

Even If This Chapter of Your Life Isn't Your Favorite, It's Also **Not Your Final**. Keep Going!

CHAPTER SEVEN

Don't Rush Brain Surgery

"It is very difficult for the prosperous to be humble."

— Jane Austen

Success is very deceptive. Just a little of it can leave you feeling like you've arrived when you haven't. This is why finding a little success is sometimes the very reason a person fails to finish reaching their goals. They either accept it as "enough" and quit, or they turn up the drive and crash. I'm admittedly guilty of making both mistakes in the past.

If you've experienced crashing or quitting before reaching your goals in the past, I have great news! There is a simple way to completely avoid repeating that experience. With this new approach, you move toward your goals in a way that sets you up to bypass both crashing or quitting through a game-changing shift in perspective. Let's dive in.

REFINING THE GIFT

When coaching or counseling people, especially young adults, I often have to remind them that life is not a race, it's a gift that is meant to be shared with others. Our parents gave us the gift of life, our friends give us the gift of friendship, and on it goes.

As you take small steps toward your goals, you are slowly cutting away what you recognize as unhealthy or unhelpful. In its place, you are transplanting, at the neurological level, what you know could and should be there. In other words, you are refining the gift that you are to the people you love and the people you encounter. This is not a process that should be rushed.

I've heard so many stories of young women who feel that they are behind in life because their friends have gotten married before they have, or young men who feel like failures because they are not making the dollar amount they expected to by a certain age. These are the most common reasons, but there are certainly others. Regardless of the reason, they feel rushed to reach their goals and often make poor decisions as a result.

A great example of this is novice runners who aim to *win* a marathon instead of simply *finishing* the marathon. This leads the runner to try to outrun the others by forcing a faster pace that ultimately burns them out, or worse, damages their health before they ever see the finish line. The physical damage that can come from such a mistake often lengthens the time it takes for them to recover and start running again.

See, unlike the 100-meter sprint, rushing is not the way to victory in a marathon. The potential damage of rushing the process often puts you further back than where you started. My point is this: the journey to your goals is not a race. Instead, it is more like brain surgery, and

THIS JOURNEY YOU'RE ON IS NOT A RACE, IT'S MORE LIKE BRAIN SURGERY.

you are on the operating table. There's a reason no one *ever* rushes brain surgery, and I don't think you want to be the first to make that mistake.

THE TEMPTATION

Separate from writing this book, I have a personal goal of writing 500 words a day. Most days I easily hit my goal almost without effort. More recently, I easily hit more than 2,000 words a day. The temptation is that I should boost my new minimum to at least 1,000 words, right? Wrong. Very, very wrong. I'll tell you why.

Increasing my minimum may seem like the natural next step, but it isn't. Boosting my minimum is only a setup for the rare occasions where I find that doing even 500 words is a struggle. It's a commitment at that moment to not give myself grace on the days when I may need it the most. And the demotivating experience attached to that lack of grace is a momentum killer on the journey to your goals.

It is important to understand this because, as you develop consistency with taking small steps toward your goals, a weird combination of things begins to happen. First, as previously mentioned, you will find that you want to do more than just take your small step, like writing 800 words instead of 500. This is a great thing, and you should maximize it by going for it.

The second thing that happens is that, as you begin to consistently do more, you may start to judge and guilt yourself by feeling like your surplus should be your new minimum aim. For example, if your small step is one push-up a day, but you've done twenty-five consistently for a week, you will be tempted to feel that you need to bump your minimum to twenty-five, but don't do it.

Start small and *stay* small until you reach your goal. This deceptive internal shift from celebrating your small wins to judging yourself for not doing more is the beginning of quitting or crashing before reaching your goal. You build momentum through consistency, not intensity. You can overthrow the temptation to increase the goal as you achieve more by choosing to celebrate the margin instead.

CELEBRATE THE MARGIN

Now when you go over your goal, instead of raising your minimum, celebrate the margin. This is a game-changing shift in perspective! Doing this will allow you to keep your minimum (500 words, 1 push-up, etc.) while celebrating a greater margin each day.

I keep my small step at 500 words daily, but I get excited about the possibility of doing more than 1,500 words in surplus. I always want to grow that margin—1,000, 1,500, 2,500, and so on. However, keeping my small step allows me to give myself the grace of just showing up when that's all I can do, without forfeiting my ambition to push my limits as I grow. We'll talk more about the importance of just showing up in the next chapter.

The hesitancy that most people have about the idea of choosing to stay small is that they see it as a lack of ambition or a fear of failure. The truth is that it's neither. Instead, it's the ability to embrace your ambitions fully, while still being able to give grace to your humanity in your moments of weakness.

A PAINFUL LESSON

My most prominent experience with this is my journey toward a physically healthier lifestyle. I mentioned briefly in the introduction that I've navigated a health condition called sickle cell anemia my entire life. Sickle cell anemia is a blood disorder that makes it easy for clots to form throughout the body, resulting in severe chronic pain.

This reality played a big part in my draw toward the arts and science as a child in place of sports. I've always been conscious of my health limitations as a result of sickle cell; however, I'm very stubborn and don't take well to feeling limited. Subsequently, even as a child, I pushed the limits and did my best to expand them. Sometimes my rebellion worked, but most of the time it ended painfully.

START SMALL AND STAY SMALL UNTIL YOU REACH YOUR GOAL.

For example, in college I decided that it was time to get fit. I wasn't overweight; on the contrary, my insecurity was that I felt smaller than I wanted to be. Doing my best to be smart about my new goal, I reached out to my friend Justin, who had recently become a certified personal trainer. Justin and I had been friends since middle school, so he was well aware of my health limitations and helped me create a plan that was perfect for me.

After about eight weeks of following the plan, I felt stronger, more energetic, and started to see results I was excited about. This taste of success made me feel like it was time to push a little harder in hopes of expediting the journey to my goal, even though that was not the plan. Big mistake.

Breaking away from the perfect plan that Justin outlined, I increased my number of workouts per week, as well as the length of my workouts. Needless to say, within days I found myself in severe pain. That mistake episode set me back months—not fun. It was a painful lesson in staying small until I reached my goal. A lesson I won't soon forget!

EXERCISE: SIMPLE STEPS TO STAYING SMALL

1. Commit now and stick to it. The first step is to commit now that you will not increase your small step *until you reach your goal.* No matter how great of a margin you achieve over time, commit to leaving room to give yourself grace. In your workbook, sign the "Stay Small Contract." This is a simple way of keeping yourself accountable for keeping your small steps.

2. Celebrate your margin. Celebrate your margin like it's a big deal—because it is! If you aimed to walk for ten minutes a day and you did eighteen minutes, celebrate the heck out of it. Throw your hands up and thank yourself for showing up and showing off. This tells your brain to do more of this behavior.

How will you celebrate the margins? Take time to write down your answer in your workbook. We will talk more about this in the next and final section of the book.

3. When you can only do the minimum, still show up! Your presence is a gift to your goals. Never undervalue it. Always show up, even if the minimum is all you can do. We'll talk more about this in the next chapter.

Remember, your transformation is not a race or competition. It's surgery. It's your future. It's worth taking your time and refusing to give in to the pressure to rush the process.

CHAPTER EIGHT

Keeping a Promise

"Few delights can equal the mere presence of one whom we trust
entirely."
— George MacDonald

In high school, I had a close friend who, for anonymity, I'll call Ana. She lived with her dad and her mom was in and out of her life. Ana clearly still loved her mom and would get excited at her promised weekend visits. The problem was that her mom rarely kept her promise and would often fail to show up without advance notice.

It wasn't hard to see how crushed Ana was any time her mom failed to keep her promise. The further we got through high school, the less excited Ana got at her mom's promises, and eventually stopped talking about her mom almost completely. Ana's experience taught me a powerful lesson about the importance of keeping a promise.

When you fail to show up for your goals, you fail to show up for your future self. It's subtle, but the blow to your momentum is not so subtle. The commitment to always show up when you say you will is a commitment to not leave your future self hanging.

THE PENNY MOUNTAIN

The principle is simple: always show up when you say you will, even if you don't do much. If your small step is a daily ten-minute walk but you just don't think you have it in you, then aim to walk for five minutes. Whatever you do, never settle for zero.

I've nicknamed this principle *The Penny Mountain* as a visual reminder that every little bit counts. I learned early that, when building wealth, every cent that you can afford to save matters. Even a penny makes the mountain bigger. On some days you may be able to contribute thousands of dollars in a single deposit, while on others, you may only be able to contribute pennies.

The power is in recognizing that the contribution of a penny still changes the final dollar amount. In the same way, your small contribution toward your goals, especially on the days when you don't feel like you have anything to give, will still move you closer to your target. Don't count yourself out at any point.

Another way to understand the significance of this principle is to recognize that every major success is just a culmination of a lot of smaller ones. Every time you show up, even if you don't do much, you contribute a small success to the collection that will eventually lead to a bigger one. Every little bit counts!

HOW I SHOWED UP TODAY

I must confess that, as I write this, today is not one of my better days. I feel completely drained and overwhelmed from my day at work, which seemed to be filled with nothing but commentary on my performance. I've had more emotionally taxing conversations than normal with friends concerning challenges in their health and difficulties in marriages.

THE COMMITMENT TO ALWAYS SHOW UP WHEN YOU SAY YOU WILL IS A COMMITMENT TO NOT LEAVE YOUR FUTURE SELF HANGING.

While it doesn't happen often, I just don't feel like I have anything left in me to give. On top of it all, despite my best efforts, my body has been aching for a week now. Not fun. It's also 10:30 p.m. as I write this and I've been up since 5:45 a.m. My point is that I get it; some days are just hard.

Plus, let's face it, there are probably millions of people who are experiencing far more difficult days, and just as many on the opposite side. And although I honestly feel empty, the fact that you're reading this means that my feelings were lying to me, just as your feelings will lie to you. It means that there was something *more* in me, and I just had to fight a little harder to show up to this laptop and get it out.

Showing up, even when it's hard, and discovering the extra energy beneath your fatigue will give you the confidence you need to do it again, and again. So push through and show up. Add your penny to the mountain; your goals are worth it.

EXERCISE: TRAINING YOUR BRAIN

DON'T COUNT YOURSELF OUT AT ANY POINT... EVERY MAJOR SUCCESS IS JUST A CULMINATION OF A LOT OF SMALLER ONES.

Remember the habit-building cycle mentioned in Chapter Six? When you are consistent in following the steps below, you will train your brain in a new pattern of behavior (or habit). The great thing about this is that it will help to make you uncomfortable when you *don't* show up at the times you should.

That uncomfortable feeling is the indication that the **trigger** has moved from external to internal[1]. This is a great thing and what you ultimately want to happen. It means that you now naturally desire to do your small steps without an external reminder and have started to more effortlessly move toward your goals.

Here are a few simple steps to help you *show up* consistently, even when you don't feel like it. Following these steps will help to remove many of the physical and mental roadblocks to your consistency. You have already worked through some of the steps, so you'll have a head start here.

1. Write down your goals. By this point you should already have this step completed, but just in case, write down your clearly defined and measurable goals in VIDA map or your workbook. You need to get it out of your head and onto paper (physically or digitally). You need it somewhere you can see it separate from yourself.

2. Break them down to daily small steps. You should also have completed this step by this point. If not, pause and revisit the exercise questions in Chapter Six. It's important to do this for all of your goals and to have a clear picture of what your daily *small steps* toward them will be.

3. Set your triggers. Identify what will remind you when it's time to show up for your goals. Is it a digital reminder, a sticky note, a planner, VIDA map? Whatever it is, make sure it's consistent and reliable, and something that will truly get you to get up and move when it's time.

4. View your goals regularly. Please, for the love of all things good, *do not* write down your goals where you will only see them "every now and then." You might as well toss them off a cliff if you do that. Instead, use VIDA map or put them somewhere that you will see them regularly so you can act on them consistently.

5. Don't count yourself out. On the days when you feel like you're done before you can even get started (like today for me), say this out loud: "I *will* show up today, even if I don't do much." Always remember that when you don't think you have much more to give, you still have at least 20% more in you.

6. Plan around your goal. Your small steps toward your goals may be small steps, but they are big priorities. As priorities, they should get priority placement in your day if possible. That means allocating your prime energy and time to them if that's within your control to do. When do you have the most energy or uninterrupted time? Prioritize taking your small steps during these times.

Doing the above will make taking your daily small steps much easier and cause you to do more over time naturally. It will help you get closer to your goals without as much resistance or effort, and your margins will naturally grow along the way.

The next and final section of this book is focused on helping you to maintain long-term success on this journey. This means moving beyond merely reaching your goals and establishing practices that will maintain life balance and enable you to enjoy the fullness of your goals when you reach them.

Part Three

Secrets For The Long Game

PART THREE OVERVIEW

SECRETS FOR THE LONG GAME

As we enter the final section of the book, it's time to turn our attention to the long game. We will take a look at what it means to live a successful life beyond reaching your goals, by establishing the four principles necessary to sustain long-term success.

It's wonderful to have strategies that can get you to your goal; however, the journey isn't over when you reach your goal. Most people make the mistake of stopping there, only to regress somehow and end up right back where they started. However, with the four principles of maintaining long-term success, it doesn't have to be that way.

Establishing these principles in your life will take time and intentionality, but when you do establish them, they change everything. You will begin to feel like your goals are chasing you, instead of the other way around. These principles are what separate those who are abundantly successful from those who are just trying to get by.

CHAPTER NINE

Adding Strategy to Celebrations

"Success consists of going from failure to failure without loss of enthusiasm."

— Winston Churchill

Many people understand celebration in the traditional way we're all introduced to it—as something to do on special occasions and when we win, right? Well, yes, but that's not the full story. When done strategically, the act of celebrating is also a powerful tool in the world of personal growth and neurological (re)programming. A strategic celebration can be used as a quick win that reminds you and your brain that the work was worth it. Let's take a closer look at what this means for us on the journey to our goals.

A different way of understanding strategic celebrations is seeing them as positive reinforcements. These are simple ways of telling your brain and body that what you are doing is a good thing, and it should resist less when you are doing it. Consider them the "Scooby Snacks" of habit formation. In this way, strategic celebrations also fall into the *reward* part of the habit-building cycle, as a form of encouragement.

According to research by Y. Joel Wong, a professor at Indiana University Bloomington who specializes in positive psychology, "Effective encouragement messages tend to emphasize process (*action*) oriented factors."[1] In other words, when encouraging yourself or others, focus on the work that was done or is going to be done. Say things like, "I'm so proud that I pushed through and *finished that chapter* instead of giving up when I felt like it. Well done!"

> "NO PROFIT GROWS WHERE THERE IS NO PLEASURE TAKEN"
> — WILLIAM SHAKESPEARE, THE TAMING OF THE SHREW[3]

Anchoring the encouragement to action gives it substance and meaning, and allows your brain to establish a connection between the action (finishing a chapter) and a positive feeling, instead of just saying, "You did well!" which is a statement that does not clearly define *what* was done well, failing to help your brain to make a clear and strong connection.

ADDING STRATEGY TO CELEBRATIONS

When it comes to strategic celebrations or positive reinforcement, intentionality is key. Hence, *strategic*. There are two things to consider that improve the effectiveness of strategic celebrations.

1. Timing is Everything. Utah State University published a behavioral guidelines checklist revealing that positive reinforcement works best directly after the task being reinforced[2]. The shorter the time, the better. This allows the brain to make an easier connection between the action and the reward.

I make it a habit to celebrate as soon as I complete the final sentence in every writing session. By doing this, I tell my brain that this celebration is directly connected to that action. I'll explain exactly how I celebrate in the next section.

2. Avoid Accidental Reinforcements. There are times when we fail to meet our daily goal and, in an attempt to make ourselves feel better, we can accidentally reinforce behaviors that we do not want to keep. It's at times like these when we say things like, "Well, that's good enough for today, I guess!" This gives our brain the wrong message!

Instead, what we may need to say is, "It sucks I didn't meet my goal. I wonder what I could have done differently?" This clearly articulates that you're not pleased with the action without beating yourself up. It leaves room for you to truly consider how you could have done things differently to reach your goal.

My personal celebration at the end of each writing session is meaningful to me, and I make sure I do it as genuinely as I can each time. Don't laugh, but this is what I do. I lift both fists in the air and declare, "*Yes!* I've slain another dragon!"

This has deep meaning to me because I picture the roadblocks to me reaching my writing goals as dragons. Every time I complete a piece of writing, therefore, I remind myself that I've slain another dragon who intended to keep me from my goal. I am *the* dragon slayer, in my head.

MY STRUGGLE WITH CELEBRATIONS

As a perfectionist, I am very committed to progress, growth, and personal development. It is my natural leaning to search for and engage in ways to improve myself, my work, and sometimes even those around me, which isn't always a great thing. Just ask my wife!

That being the case, it's no surprise that I struggle with strategic celebration and have to be a bit more intentional than most. My disposition drives me to look for the next thing to work on, instead of naturally wanting to take a moment to celebrate the completion of the last thing. This is where self-awareness was a great asset for me and could be for you as well, not just for strategic celebrations, but for all the principles in this section of the book.

Having an understanding of my personality, and learning the power and importance of strategic celebration, made for a great catalyst for intentionality. While I struggle with celebrations in this way, I knew that my wife and a few close friends, on the other hand, did not. They tend to be great at celebrating, and even better at getting me to pause and celebrate.

So, in addition to finding a pronounced way to celebrate immediately after completing a small step, I will sometimes text my wife or reach out to a friend and share what I've done. This allows me to reinforce the positive behavior and build momentum toward my goals.

EXERCISE: CELEBRATING MEANINGFULLY

Here are four ways that you can celebrate meaningfully when you accomplish your daily small steps. You can use these ideas to get started and build on them as you discover what works best for you. The more meaningful and personal the celebration is, the better.

THANK YOURSELF FOR SHOWING UP. YOU CHOSE NOT TO LEAVE YOUR GOALS HANGING AND THAT'S WORTH SOME APPRECIATION.

1. Say Thank You. You can thank yourself for showing up. You chose not to leave your goals hanging, and that's worth some appreciation. You can say "thank you" out loud, write a thank you note, or use some other method. You can also use a combination of ways to keep it fresh. However you choose to do it, make it something you look forward to doing for yourself.

2. Document The Success. Write down what you did and why it's meaningful. If you completed a workout, write it down and then write why it's a big deal. Don't be shy about it; allow yourself to be honored in the accomplishment.

If documenting the success is what works best for you, consider buying a journal. Having a journal that's filled with just your successes and why they matter to you could be a very healing gift to yourself. Get a nice one that you will be excited to fill!

3. Give Meaningful Rewards. If giving yourself a gift is what gets you excited, then get to gift-giving! I know of one writer whose gift to themself for being faithful to their morning routine is a latte. It is a reward they make themself earn, then take time to enjoy it when they do.

Consider making a list of gifts you can "earn" for yourself with each success. It could be the same each time, like a latte, or a different gift each time that gets better with each successful day. Don't hold back!

4. Public Recognition. Talk to someone about what you have accomplished. Don't wait for them to acknowledge that it's a great thing; instead, say something like, "Man, I'm so proud of myself for doing x" out loud to someone. Most people respond with more encouragement to that, anyway.

You can make a list of people you like and trust to celebrate with, people who can understand and encourage you as you make progress. Your celebration partner could also be a complete stranger in a Starbucks somewhere who you strike up a conversation with. Whatever floats your boat!

In your workbook, take the time to write out what form of encouragement means the most to you and why. Who does it usually come from? Why does their voice matter most to you? Answering these and the other questions in your workbook will help you to discover how to celebrate yourself meaningfully.

CHAPTER TEN

Boosting Your Mental Health

"Just because you don't understand it doesn't mean it isn't so."
— **Lemony Snicket, The Blank Book**

Cultivating great mental health is the second principle for sustaining long-term success. Keep in mind that sustained success depends on being healthy on all levels. Ignoring your mental health while growing healthy in other areas is like having a party on the top deck of a cruise while ignoring the hole in the bottom of the boat, assuming that because the party is still going on that nothing is wrong. Eventually, the boat will sink.

A healthy and sharp mind is one of the greatest defenses

against poor decision-making, poor physical health, and deteriorating relationships. It helps you to see and receive the ugly truth, which most people choose to ignore. Then it helps you to process that truth and make the hard decisions that are best for you, your future, and the people around you.

This chapter outlines simple steps that you can take to cultivate great mental health as you work toward your goals.

UNDERSTANDING MENTAL HEALTH

When I worked as a pastor, I often found myself counseling people who were navigating poor mental health. However, most people had no idea that what they were dealing with was a mental health issue because of some common misconceptions, some of which I was personally familiar with. Moreover, it is only recently that we, as a society, have begun to recognize how broad and wide-reaching mental health really is.

Many people that I sat with often only saw mental health issues as serious meltdowns, severe depression, and anxiety. While these things are very much a part of mental health, it is important to recognize that they are a part of a broad spectrum. In truth, mental health is connected to other more common experiences like stress, focus, fatigue, excessive busyness, lack of motivation, and much more.[1]

Have you ever wondered why professional sports organizations, teams, and even individual athletes have chaplains, therapists, and physical trainers on hand? It is because they understand that the game they play is physical, but in order to win and *keep winning,* they need to be healthy on all levels. This includes keeping their mental game sharp so they can focus and perform at their best, especially under pressure.

YOU SHOULD SEE A THERAPIST

I remember the first time my wife recommended that I see a therapist. In the past, she had found it to be personally helpful, and she thought it could be helpful to me. Insightfully, she recognized that there was potential for me to grow as a leader and that there might be some unseen hurdles holding me back. She wasn't wrong, but the recommendation caught me off guard.

To be honest, I was highly offended. I did not grow up in a culture where therapy was the norm or even talked about. I, like some of those I counseled, saw it as only necessary under extreme circumstances. I interpreted her recommendation as an emotional dig at me.

SOMETIMES GROWING HEALTHIER MEANS GROWING SLOWER. LEARN TO BE OKAY WITH THAT.

It wasn't until about two years later that my attitude toward mental health and my wife's suggestion completely changed. The catalyst for the change was a work trip. On the trip, I heard a respected leader share about the relationship he had with his therapist and its impact on his life, health, and marriage. I heard his description through my perfectionist filter and began to see it as an opportunity for personal development, and could not unsee it in that light.

Needless to say, by the end of the trip I was committed to finding a therapist. I was finally willing to do whatever it took to grow and begin moving forward in this area of life. This was a whole new avenue for me to learn to be a better husband and leader, and I was excited about it.

Of course, there was also the issue of any un-dealt-with trauma in my life that was holding me back as a husband, friend, and leader, which, when I began to address it, catapulted me forward. I've since become a strong advocate for therapy when it's appropriate, as well as helped others determine if it is right for them.

If you find that the hurdles to improving your mental health are deeper than a few adjustments to your diet or physical exercise, it may be worthwhile to seek the counsel of a licensed therapist. Sometimes the tools we need for the growth we want sit in someone else's tool kit. Whether that's a pastor, therapist, life coach, or mentor, we need to step out of our comfort zone and into their expertise.

BOOSTING YOUR MENTAL HEALTH QUICKLY

My first attempt at seeking to improve my mental health, however, started in a conversation with my doctor, long before my wife's recommendation. At the time, I was struggling with insomnia, lack of focus, and a really bad memory... like, really, really bad memory. To my surprise, my doctor didn't recommend a new drug or a different diet. He shared some simple, easy, and free things that are often overlooked when it comes to brain health.

What I share with you below includes what he suggested, as well as a few strategies that I learned along the way. Applying any one of these can improve your mental health. Applying all of them has the potential to change your life. I will also note here that **I am not** a dietician or medical professional. Before making any serious changes to your diet or physical activity, please check with a trusted medical professional who knows your health concerns.

1. Limit Interaction with Toxic People. This is one of the most beneficial things you can do for your mental health. Toxic people are called "toxic" for a reason. Do not let any toxic person "slide."

Using the exercise in your workbook, you can create a circle of influence and circle of concern. The circle of influence includes people who you want to influence you and your future. The circle of concern is for people you care about but who are not healthy enough to be allowed that kind of influence in your life.

2. Take Control of Your Tech. Many of us own a lot of technology that, over time, begins to own us. We allow things like notifications, emails, and even the shows we watch to dictate our calendars and actions. Taking control of your tech allows you to create the kind of environment that your mind can flourish in.

There are simple things that you can do to address this, such as turning off notifications for non-essential apps and setting

FEAR CAN MAKE YOU MOVE, BUT RARELY IN THE RIGHT DIRECTION. DON'T PUT FEAR IN THE DRIVER'S SEAT.

reminders for when you want to check them. Social media is perhaps the most important category to apply this action to. Instead of feeling glued to your device and triggered by a lit-up screen or a vibration, you will regain control over what and when information comes into your life. I suggest doing the same for things like emails as well, unless your job demands otherwise.

3. Read Regularly. This suggestion will excite some people, and others may just skip it, and that's okay. However, a simple way to keep your mind sharp is by exercising it. Reading allows you to do this. Listening to a book does the same thing, though to a far lesser extent. Studies confirm that reading regularly helps to reduce stress, fights depression symptoms, prevents cognitive decline as you age, and much more.[2]

I suggest finding topics you are passionate about and reading a short book on them. Even if you only read five minutes a day, you'll see a big difference in your mental sharpness over time. Create a reading list for each year and work your way through that list in your free time.

4. Eat Brain Food. No, brain food is not a brand. However, there are plenty of foods that carry extra benefits for the brain. A simple google search can help you to identify a few that you like that will work for your diet.

These "brain foods" range from snacks like nuts and dark chocolate to fish like salmon and trout. Other food items like blueberries and turmeric are included on the list. For additional reading, check out the book *Brain Food* by Dr. Lisa Mosconi.[3]

5. Physical Activity. While I understand that not everyone can be as mobile as they like due to potential medical conditions, the goal here is to introduce regular physical activity into your routine. A simple fifteen to twenty-minute walk is usually more than enough.

Physical activity gets your heart pumping healthy amounts of blood and oxygen throughout your body, including your brain. That's why Bill Gates plays tennis regularly in hopes of keeping his brain sharp[4]. I choose to go for a two-mile walk each morning.

6. Journal Daily. While it is probably less popular than reading and physical activity for most, journaling is a therapeutic way of dealing with the things your brain carries around but doesn't tell you about. It allows you to discover the things that weigh you down that you may not even know are there.

There's an exercise by author Julia Cameron called "Morning Pages" that got me into journaling daily back in college[5]. Before this exercise, I *never* liked to journal. This amazing exercise is outlined in more detail on Julia's website, www.juliacameronlive.com. See your workbook for more information.

7. Learn an Instrument or Language. This suggestion is for those who want to take their brain health to another level. The activity of learning a new instrument or a new language is one of the ultimate exercises of the brain. It forces your neurons to create new connections and causes you to think in different and more creative ways, among other benefits[6].

There are many ways to learn an instrument or a language cheap or for free. YouTube is the first option that comes to mind. I share more ideas in the workbook on different ways to get started on this part of your journey.

While it isn't free, I listen to a language-learning software on my morning walks. This allows my brain to soak up the information more easily and helps me to retain more. I'm currently learning the Italian language. To create your mental health master list, see the workbook section associated with this chapter.

In Life,

Experience Is

Guaranteed

But **Growth** Is

A Choice.

CHAPTER ELEVEN

Synergetic Life Balance

"The trick to balance is to not make sacrificing important things become
the norm."

— Simon Sinek

The third principle in sustaining long-term success is also the
hardest. It's the ability to maintain a sense of balance across the
four areas of life. As a reminder, those areas are our personal life,
family life, social life, and career life. The absence of a sense of
balance in life is the root cause of many failed marriages, parental
gaps, moral failures, and of course, failed goals.

It is also important to note that when I use the word
"balance," I'm referring to a synergetic relationship between the

four areas of life and not an equal distribution of time and energy across them. Aiming for an equal distribution of time and energy across all areas of life is disastrous and will keep true balance perpetually out of reach.

In contrast, synergetic balance, which is the cooperative interaction of the four areas, allows for the kind of flexibility our complicated lives need. Synergy recognizes that different stages of life require varying levels of attention from us in each area. A great example of this is the distinction between what a balanced life for a single working professional looks like, compared to a balanced life for a married mom with preteens. Each area of life demands very different things from these individuals as a result of their stage of life.

> *WORK-LIFE BALANCE IS NOT ONE SIZE FITS ALL. IT NEVER WAS.*

If you want to find synergetic balance in life, the key question to ask is, "What does an improved quality of life look like for me in this season?" A clear answer to this question often reveals what each area of life will need to look like to achieve that improved quality of life.

THE MYTH OF TIME MANAGEMENT

A critical roadblock to achieving synergetic balance in life is one of the longest-standing myths of the twenty-first century—the myth of time management. One of the most popular recommendations to people who desire to improve their quality of life is to get better at time management. While the idea may work for a few, it fails quickly for many others because its foundation is flawed.

Upon further inspection, you will find the idea of time management to be ludicrous, no matter how it's spun. Time is a force that is untouched and untouchable by humanity. The only true manipulation of time throughout history has always been our perspective of it.

In reality, time flows at its own pleasing and does not respond to our demands. Think about it: we cannot slow time down to relish a precious moment with a loved one, and we cannot speed it up, no matter how hard we try, during the embarrassing, unpleasant, or painful moments in life. If that were possible, I'm certain someone would have fast-forwarded through the year 2020! How then do we manage a force that we cannot control? The answer? We can't.

Additionally, trying to control something that is out of your control is the primary ingredient to things like stress, anxiety, and depression. If you want to improve your life balance, choose instead to start managing your priorities. Unlike time, your priorities are within your control. Plus it is your responsibility to identify and manage your priorities anyway.

You manage your priorities by first identifying what they are, then identifying their level of importance in light of the rest of your life, and finally determining the amount of focus and attention they require. Choosing when, where, how, and for how long you focus your attention on any given task or relationship is a reflection of your priorities above all else. For help identifying your priorities, revisit your answers to the questions at the end of Chapter One.

FIRST THINGS FIRST

When I was a young artist, I often dreamed of having an elaborate recording studio filled with the best equipment on the market. I would digitally window-shop and imagine a future when I would create my art in such a space. I later learned that obsession with a specific microphone, interface, or mixer is common with many artists at that stage of their journey.

If I could go back in time and advise the younger me, I would explain how misguided my focus was and encourage him to return to what mattered most: the finished product. The truth is that people have used lesser-quality tools to create great art throughout history. An obsession with the tool, in place of the finished product, was only a distraction.

A common mistake that causes life balance to stay out of reach is making balance itself the goal. Making life balance your goal is the equivalent of the younger me obsessing over a microphone instead of the music. Like the microphone, life balance is a tool meant to assist you in reaching greater goals, and not meant to be the goal itself.

A balanced life provides the breathing room necessary for you to move actively toward your greater potential. When you are stressed out from poor self-care, family drama, an overwhelming work schedule, or having no social life, you do not have the capacity to grow your potential in any significant way. Additionally, being stressed out by one area without the relief that should come from the others often leads to poor decision-making and moral, relational, or financial ruin, as mentioned in the previous chapter.

> *TIME IS NOT OURS TO MANAGE, BUT OUR PRIORITIES ARE!*

However, when you have balance in life, you are free to dream up greater futures for you, your loved ones, and even the world. More importantly, you will also have the emotional and mental capacity to act on those dreams, which is one of the superpowers of a balanced life.

GOING THE EXTRA MILE

The question, then, is how do we improve and maintain our life balance without making it the goal or an obsession? For the Bill Gates and Jeff Bezos of the world, there are assistants, entire management teams, and much more to keep a watch on all the priority pieces of their lives. But what about you? How will you maintain balance and keep track of the most important things in your life?

Below are a few ways to go the extra mile in discovering, developing, and maintaining synergetic balance in life. You can find more details in your workbook.

1. Track Your Energy. Do you know where your best energy is going? Is it to work, or with family? It's possible to ensure that you still give your best at work while reserving enough energy to be fully present at home as well. In the same way that you track your finances with a budget, you can use VIDA map or another tool to track your best energy as well. Craig Groeschel calls this practice The Art of Energy Management[1].

2. Drop the Ball. Many people are often trying to juggle too many things at once, and they know it. The badge of busyness is too great an achievement to give up for some reason. These are the folks who also struggle with saying "no." The reality is that some things driving you up a wall are things you could choose to stop doing, and it would not impact your life in any meaningful way.

3. Start with No. This is an exercise based on the idea we looked at in Chapter Two on ways to narrow your focus. Learn to say "no" can be an easy way to lighten the load of an overbooked calendar. If you struggle with saying "no," try doing this. For one month, when you are asked to do something or go somewhere, make your default answer a strong "no," unless you absolutely must. The goal is to practice the art of creating breathing room or blank spaces in your calendar.

I also find it helpful to say these reminders out loud sometimes.

"'No' is a full sentence. I don't always need to explain why." "Saying 'no' is not a sin." "Every time I say 'yes' to something, I am saying 'no' to something else. I must make sure it's worth it." "My time is a limited resource and should be used wisely."

4. Minimize Distractions at Work. Minimizing distractions at work is key to maximizing your time at home and elsewhere. Being more productive at work means being free from the nagging thoughts of unfinished projects, or worse, actually taking work home. Start making strategic decisions to improve your efficiency at work.

CHAPTER TWELVE

Finding Your Tribe

"Finding your tribe can have transformative effects on your sense of identity and purpose."

— **Sir. Ken Robinson, The Element**

The fourth and final principle of sustaining long-term success is finding and joining your *tribe*. In this context, a tribe is a community of like-minded people who share your passion, goal, or skill and can join you on your journey. In other words, people who *get it*. This is one of the most impactful decisions for every goal-getter when we apply our understanding of selective syncing.

I first came across the idea and significance of finding my tribe through the late author, speaker, and education reformer Sir

Ken Robinson. Sir Robinson's TED Talk currently holds the record for the most-watched TED Talk of all time with over 65 million views at the time of this writing[1]. I confess that I am probably personally responsible for about one million of those views.

THE TED TALK

I remember it like it was yesterday. In my freshman year of college, one of my professors, who is now a great friend, showed the video of Robinson's talk in class. I was entranced, completely captivated by every word Robinson shared.

Robinson talked about education reform with candor, comedy, evidence, and conviction, but that's not what changed my life. Toward the end of his talk, he told the story of a young woman who struggled in school as a child. She couldn't focus, fidgeted a lot, and her teacher was ready to give up on her.

> *TRIBE MEMBERS CAN BE COLLABORATORS OR COMPETITORS.*
> - SIR KEN ROBINSON, THE ELEMENT

The teacher deemed her effectively deficient and told her mom to take her to a psychologist. The concerned mom did, and the brilliant psychologist diagnosed the child as completely fine, just out of place.

The psychologist suggested that the child be enrolled in a school for dancers and, needless to say, she flourished. The child's name was Gillian Lynne. She grew up to be an award-winning ballerina and choreographer who helped to make several Broadway shows like *Phantom of the Opera* and *Cats* possible[2]. All because she found her tribe. She found a place where she was surrounded by people who understood how she was naturally wired and what she desired to do.

On your journey to your goals, there are times you may feel alone or ostracized because of your determination or approach. Let this be an encouragement to you that you may be completely fine, just out of place.

FINDING MY TRIBE

After seeing this video, I purchased Sir Ken Robinson's best-selling book *The Element*[3] that day. In it, he explains what it means to discover your element and find your tribe. He also shares many other inspirational stories. If you are looking for more stories like Gillian's to motivate you, I highly recommend this book.

Learning the significance of a tribe completely changed how I approached my personal growth and goals in whatever field I found myself. As I was launching my professional music career, I immediately applied the idea and found my tribe. My independent music career became like no other.

As a result of finding my tribe, I was able to do some amazing things throughout my music career. I toured the East Coast of the US. I launched a record label with a major distribution deal with Sony RED and worked with a management team in Nashville that also managed some other amazing artists. I also used this principle as a small business and label owner.

When I moved on from music and entered pastoral ministry and leadership, I applied the principle again. I joined a group of student ministry pastors who met monthly to connect and encourage each other. I grew exponentially from their experiences, stories, friendship, and the opportunity to work together with them.

Now, as an author and entrepreneur, I've entered back into a season of finding, and now building, my tribe. It's exciting and motivating to connect with like-minded people who understand my journey. These are people who can connect with my successes and struggles, and we also encourage each other along the way.

FINDING YOUR TRIBE

Finding your tribe doesn't need to be complicated or intimidating. There are a few things to look for as you find your tribe and determine if they're the right fit for you. In my experience, I found three things, in particular, to be most important: passion, goal, and skill. The people in your tribe should share any or all three of these things.

1. Your Passion. When I was an artist, I participated in a benefit concert that Katie, a friend of mine, hosted in the wake of

Superstorm Sandy. She organized graphic designers, musicians, dancers, and craft-makers around her passion, and we worked together for months to pull it off. We didn't share the same skill sets, but we shared her passion for helping those in need.

2. Your Goal. Your tribe may be a group of people who share your goal. When I worked with Katie for her benefit concert, we also shared a goal: to raise money for families with young children who were in need. This is also what happens when we join a class at a gym filled with others who share a goal of losing weight or getting healthy.

3. Your Skill. Your tribe can consist of people who share your skill. As a hip-hop artist, I was surrounded by others who shared the skill of writing and producing music. We encouraged, energized, and challenged each other to grow and hone our skills. In this sense, your tribe can even be a group of people you compete with.

What I call the Golden Triangle is when you find a tribe who share all three of these things with you. That's a community that has the potential to catapult you toward your goals and ultimately your *destiny* or *calling*. This is always my goal when looking for a tribe, but it's not always possible or easy to find.

Use the activity questions in your workbook to discover where you might be able to find a tribe around you or online.

BENEFITS OF A TRIBE

While there are many benefits to joining a tribe, there are a few that are certainly worth mentioning. Listed below are the top reasons, in my opinion, to invest time in finding and joining a tribe.

1. Synergy. Joining a tribe creates synergy toward your goals. The community momentum makes personal progress require less energy. This is worth investing in any day.

> *FINDING YOUR TRIBE OFFERS MORE THAN VALIDATION AND INTERACTION... IT PROVIDES INSPIRATION AND PROVOCATION TO RAISE THE BAR ON YOUR OWN ACHIEVEMENTS.*
>
> *- SIR KEN ROBINSON, THE ELEMENT*

2. Encouragement. A tribe is an amazing source of encouragement and inspiration. It can help you to "see the light" and not give up when you hit the inevitable low points that come with every journey. This is especially important if, after filtering your friends, there aren't many left to support or encourage you.

3. Accountability. Tribes are great for accountability because your success is everyone's success. When one person in the tribe begins to slip, the entire tribe is invested in helping them recover. They become a sort of guardrail along the way to your goal.

4. BONUS: They "get it." The greatest benefit to finding and joining a tribe is probably the fact that they are a group of people who "get it." This means they will probably be the one group of people who you simply never have to explain your struggle to because they're walking it with you, and they understand. They can give you a unique sense of validation on your journey that's unachievable anywhere else.

This is the equivalent of a group of athletes commenting on each other's performance. They'll have inside language, gestures, and even grace for each other that others who aren't on the team just won't get. It's a part of why runner's clubs, knitting clubs, and writing groups exist.

JOIN MY TRIBE

I've created a free online community for goal-getters who embrace the life balance approach to goal-getting. It's a community for people who've read this book and understand the mentality of small steps in the right direction. People who understand the times when you want to celebrate the fact that you still "showed up" and it's a big deal, even though you only did five push-ups or only wrote five sentences.

If you would like to join this community, you can do so today. To join this community visit www.paulwcroswell.com/groups and then select "The Life Balance Tribe". This is an exclusive community only for those who've gone through this book and are ready to find their tribe. See you there!

Bi Sheng's Story

Allow me to share one last story with you as you complete this milestone in your journey.

Very little is known about Bi Sheng, a Chinese inventor who lived roughly from 970 AD to 1051 AD, but personally, I would love to go back and shake his hand if it were possible. Sheng, who was from Yingshan, Hubei, China, invented the very first reusable movable type.[1] His invention became the first of its kind, allowing him to produce early forms of print documents in a world where everyone still documented information and stories by hand.

Sheng's movable type became an early forerunner for the Gutenberg printing press, invented almost 400 years later by Johannes Gutenberg in 1450. The popularization of the printing press is almost directly responsible for the growth of literacy, education, and mass availability of uniform information for ordinary people.[2] The ripple effect of Bi Sheng reaching his goal is incomprehensible, but its significance here is far more personal.

Sheng had no idea that reaching his goal of inventing a reusable movable type would impact the life of a young man from Portmore, Jamaica centuries later, but it did. I am that young man, and I'm grateful that he did not give up on his goal because it created the circumstances that made my dream of becoming an author possible. What I find more powerful is that it doesn't stop there. Bi Sheng is included on a list of potentially millions of people who, by reaching their goals, make the circumstances of our lives and dreams possible today.

Now, in pursuit of my own goal of becoming an author, I'm helping to make your goals possible by sharing ideas that I hope will help you go further faster. I say all of this to emphasize that you have no idea what the ripple effects of reaching your goals will be, of the lives you may touch and improve as a result of it. I sincerely hope you do not give up on reaching your goals.

YOU ARE A GIFT

Finally, congratulations! You've taken a massive leap toward improving your life balance and reaching your goals by completing this book. This is no small task, and I hope you take the time to celebrate it well. As you continue on your way to your goals and a happier future, remember that life is not a race, it's a gift—a gift that's meant to be shared with others. You are a gift to this world, and each step you take toward your goal refines that gift just a little bit more.

Always remember, a small step in the right direction is a big deal.

An Important Note

If this book has helped you on your journey to your goals and a better life balance, you can help to spread the word about it by telling others about or reading through it with a group. Your recommendation of this book to a friend or colleague is the highest form of compliment to its impact on your life. You can also tell me about your experience with this book by visiting www.paulwcroswell.com and sharing your story. Your story may be the inspiration someone else needs in order to start transforming their own.

About The Author

Paul W. Croswell is a life-balance coach for young professionals and the creator of VIDA map, the work-life balance manager. Based in central New Jersey, he hosts The Pocket Potential Podcast and a personal development blog called READ'R by Paul W Croswell. Paul has spent almost a decade learning to tap into the power of life balance and now he teaches young professionals how to use it to reach their most intimidating goals, improve their personal growth, and live deeply meaningful lives. Connect with Paul at www.paulwcroswell.com or on social media (@paulwcroswell).

Bibliography

Introduction

1 Norcross, J C, and D J Vangarelli. "The resolution solution: longitudinal examinations of New Year's change attempts." *Journal of substance abuse* vol. 1,2 (1988): 127-34. doi:10.1016/s0899-3289(88)80016-6

2 Garton, Eric. "Employee Burnout Is a Problem with the Company, Not the Person." *Harvard Business Review*, 20 July 2017, hbr.org/2017/04/employee-burnout-is-a-problem-with-the-company-not-the-person.

3 McGuirk, Rod. "Australia Plans $190 Billion Defense Boost over Decade." *Tribune*, San Diego Union-Tribune, 1 July 2020, www.sandiegouniontribune.com/business/nation/story/2020-06-30/australia-plans-190-billion-defense-boost-over-decade.

4 MacKay, Jory. "The State of Work Life Balance in 2019 (According to Data) - RescueTime." *RescueTime Blog*, 8 May 2019, blog.rescuetime.com/work-life-balance-study-2019/.

Chapter Two

1 Clear, James. "How to Focus Better: Lessons From a Lion Tamer." *James Clear*, 4 Feb. 2020, jamesclear.com/how-to-focus.

2 Blaschka, Amy. "This Is Why Saying 'No' Is The Best Way To Grow Your Career-And How To Do It." *Forbes*, Forbes Magazine, 26 Nov. 2019, www.forbes.com/sites/amyblaschka/2019/11/26/this-is-why-saying-no-is-the-best-way-to-grow-your-career-and-how-to-do-it/#13aa35d3479d.

3 Dinsmore, Scott. "01 Feb Warren Buffett's 5-Step Process for Prioritizing True Success (and Why Most People Never Do It)." *Live*

Your Legend, 1 Feb. 1970, liveyourlegend.net/warren-buffetts-5-step-process-for-prioritizing-true-success-and-why-most-people-never-do-it/.

Chapter Three

[1] Stanley, Andy. *Guardrails: Avoiding Regrets in Your Life.* Zondervan, 2011.

[2] Johnson, George Clayton, et al. "Ocean's Eleven." *IMDb*, Warner Bros, 7 Dec. 2001, www.imdb.com/title/tt0240772/.

[3] Koppelman, Brian, and David Levien. "Ocean's Thirteen." *IMDb*, Warner Bros, 5 June 2007, www.imdb.com/title/tt0496806/.

[4] FeaturedOpen Neuroscience ArticlesPsychology·August 28, 2020·4 min read, et al. "Our Brains Synchronize During Conversation." *Neuroscience News*, 20 July 2017, neurosciencenews.com/conversation-brain-synchronization-7135/.

[5] Weller, Chris. "A Neuroscientist Who Studies Decision-Making Reveals the Most Important Choice You Can Make." *Thrive Global*, 18 Aug. 2017, thriveglobal.com/stories/a-neuroscientist-who-studies-decision-making-reveals-the-most-important-choice-you-can-make/.

[6] Brené Brown, Brené. "Clear Is Kind. Unclear Is Unkind." *Brené Brown*, 21 Aug. 2019, brenebrown.com/blog/2018/10/15/clear-is-kind-unclear-is-unkind/.

Chapter Four

[1] Pincott, Jena E. "Silencing Your Inner Critic." *Psychology Today*, Sussex Publishers, 4 Mar. 2019, www.psychologytoday.com/us/articles/201903/silencing-your-inner-critic.

[2] "Ideation." *Strengthsfinder 2.0*, by Tom Rath, Gallup Press, 2017, pp. 113–116.

[3] McElroy, Shaun. "Ideation by StrengthsMining." *StrengthsMining*, 2018, www.strengthsmining.com/gallup-strengthsfinder/strategic-

thinking/ideation/.

4   Stanley, Andy. "Four Questions for Better Decisions - Part 2: 'The Story of Your Life.'" *Your Move*, 22 Jan. 2020, yourmove.is/videos/the-story-of-your-life/.

Chapter Five

1   Dictionary, Cambridge. "MAP: Definition in the Cambridge English Dictionary." *MAP | Definition in the Cambridge English Dictionary*, 1995, dictionary.cambridge.org/us/dictionary/english/map.

Chapter Six

1   Guise, Stephen. *Mini Habits: Smaller Habits, Bigger Results.* Amazon, 2013.

2   Pietrangelo, Ann. "Dopamine Effects on the Body, Plus Drug and Hormone Interactions." *Healthline*, Healthline Media, 5 Nov. 2019, www.healthline.com/health/dopamine-effects.

3   McRaven, William H. *Make Your Bed: Little Things That Can Change Your Life ... and Maybe the World.* Michael Joseph, an Imprint of Penguin Books, 2017.

4   Eyal, Nir, and Ryan Hoover. *Hooked How to Build Habit-Forming Products.* Penguin Business, 2019.

Chapter Eight

1   Toxboe, Anders, and Nir Eyal. "Nir Eyal: Trigger Users' Actions and Reward Them to Build Habits." *UI Patterns*, 3 June 2015, ui-patterns.com/blog/nir-eyal-trigger-actions-and-reward-them-to-build-habits.

Chapter Nine

1   Wong, Y. Joel. "The Psychology of Encouragement: Theory, Research, and Applications - Vol. 43(2) 178–216." *Tcp.sagepub.com*, The

Counseling Psychologist, 2015, www.apa.org/education/ce/psychology-encouragement.pdf.

2 Cherry, Kendra. "Positive Reinforcement Can Help Favorable Behaviors." *Verywell Mind*, 29 Nov. 2019, www.verywellmind.com/what-is-positive-reinforcement-2795412#citation-3.

Chapter Ten

1 Campbell, Polly. "4 Things to Do When Your Brain Is Tired." *Psychology Today*, Sussex Publishers, 9 July 2015, www.psychologytoday.com/us/blog/imperfect-spirituality/201507/4-things-do-when-your-brain-is-tired.

2 Stanborough, Rebecca Joy. "Benefits of Reading Books: For Your Physical and Mental Health." Edited by Heidi Moawad, *Healthline*, Healthline Media, 15 Oct. 2019, www.healthline.com/health/benefits-of-reading-books.

3 Mosconi, Dr. Lisa. *Brain Food*. Penguin Books Ltd., 2019.

4 Gates, Bill, et al. "Inside Bill's Brain: Decoding Bill Gates." *IMDb*, IMDb.com, 20 Sept. 2019, www.imdb.com/title/tt10837476/.

5 Cameron, Julia. *Artist's Way: 25th Anniversary Edition*. Penguin Books, 2016.

6 Skibba, Ramin. "How a Second Language Can Boost the Brain." *Knowable Magazine | Annual Reviews*, Annual Reviews, 29 Nov. 2018, www.knowablemagazine.org/article/mind/2018/how-second-language-can-boost-brain.

Chapter Eleven

1 Groeschel, Craig. "Craig Groeschel Leadership Podcast - The Art of Energy Management." *Life.Church*, 5 June 2019, www.life.church/leadershippodcast/the-art-of-energy-management/.

Chapter Twelve

1   Robinson, Sir Ken. "Do Schools Kill Creativity?" *TED*, Feb. 2006, www.ted.com/talks/sir_ken_robinson_do_schools_kill_creativity? language=en.

2   Lynne, Gillian. "GILLIAN LYNNE BIOGRAPHY." *Gillian Lynne - Biography*, 2018, www.gillianlynne.com/biography.htm.

3   Robinson, Sir Ken. *The Element: How Finding Your Passion Changes Everything*, by Ken Robinson and Lou Aronica, Penguin, 2010, pp. 103–131.

Bi Sheng's Story

1   Norman, Jeremy M. "The Invention of Movable Type in China." *The Invention of Movable Type in China: History of Information*, 25 Jan. 2012, www.historyofinformation.com/detail.php?id=19.

2   History.com Editors. "Printing Press." *History.com*, A&E Television Networks, 7 May 2018, www.history.com/topics/inventions/printing-press.

Notes